BEFORE YOU SAY
"I Do"

BEFORE YOU SAY "I DO"

Important Questions
to Ask Before Marriage

REVISED AND UPDATED

TODD OUTCALT

A Perigee Book

A PERIGEE BOOK
Published by the Penguin Group
Penguin Group (USA) LLC
375 Hudson Street, New York, New York 10014

USA • Canada • UK • Ireland • Australia • New Zealand • India • South Africa • China

penguin.com

A Penguin Random House Company

Second revised Perigee trade paperback ISBN: 978-0-399-16712-6

The Library of Congress has cataloged the original Perigee edition as follows:

Outcalt, Todd.
Before you say "I do" : important questions for couples to ask before marriage / Todd Outcalt.—1st ed.
p.   cm.
"A Perigee Book."
ISBN 0-399-52375-8
1. Marriage—Miscellanea.   2. Communication in marriage—Miscellanea.   I. Title.
HQ734.O78   1998
306.81—dc21   97-16804

PUBLISHING HISTORY
Original Perigee trade paperback edition / January 1998
Revised Perigee trade paperback edition / January 2006
Second revised Perigee trade paperback edition / January 2014

PRINTED IN THE UNITED STATES OF AMERICA

10   9   8   7   6   5   4   3   2   1

To Becky, *for the best years*

CONTENTS

ACKNOWLEDGMENTS

The creation of any book owes its existence to a great many people; I acknowledge that this is certainly the case with this third edition of *Before You Say "I Do."*

From the outset—and after thirty years of pastoral ministry—I wish to thank the many couples who have allowed me to be a part of their lives both before and after their weddings. Although I have changed the names and situations in this book at many turns, I am grateful to have so many true-life experiences to draw upon. I am also grateful to the many couples who have come to me for marital counseling—and who have taught me much about the joys and stresses of marriage.

Since the first publication of this book in 1998, I have had the privilege of speaking to many groups about marriage, and I wish to thank those who have provided me a forum for addressing one of life's greatest challenges—and joys. I also thank the many magazine editors—of bridal magazines in particular—who have published my work through the years. There have been many opportunities to learn from other couples, and I am grateful to all who have opened their hearts and their homes to me.

I am also grateful to the hundreds of couples who have written to me over the years with their questions about marriage. I have not always been able to provide answers—marriage

is, after all, a relationship of imperfections. But I have appreciated the opportunity to have a conversation with so many other
couples, and to learn from their insights and struggles and successes. Much is learned through sharing, and this book is no
different. I thank all who have shared in it.

Thank you, Cynthia, for being my advocate for this third
edition and for your tireless and consistent efforts through
the years. I look forward to other projects together and value
your insights. Thanks so much.

I am grateful this time around to Jeanette Shaw, whose
editing skills guided this new edition to final form, to the
staff at Perigee for their good work, and I am ever grateful to
John Duff, publisher, for his continuing support. Many books
don't have the longevity or the commitment—and I am
indeed grateful for the opportunity to write this third edition
and to make it available to a wider audience.

Finally, I thank my family—Chelsey, Michael, and Logan.
And I thank my wife, Becky—for thirty years of marriage, a
significant accomplishment for two imperfect people who
still love each other. We are still saying "I do"—and the best
is yet to come.

INTRODUCTION

So You Want to Get Married?

As a pastor, I have had many opportunities to counsel couples before marriage. I have helped them plan weddings big and small, guided them when one or both were having last-minute doubts, and sat beside them later at the reception.

But, in spite of the many weddings I've seen and officiated at, I never lose sight of the fact that *it is much more difficult to have a marriage than a wedding.* Anyone can organize a wedding, but not everyone can have a long and happy marriage. A wedding takes planning. Marriage requires hard work. A wedding can be had for the cost of a cake and punch bowl. A good marriage cannot be purchased in any way.

Marriage is about two unique people who decide to form a unique relationship with each other. Even though there are millions of marriages, every one of them is unique in its composition, joy, expectation, stress, partnership, sadness, and love. It has been my observation that every marriage has to stand on the strength, resiliency, and love of the two individuals.

But how, if one is considering marriage, does one determine the true strengths and weaknesses of the loved one? Is there any way to plumb the depths of another's mind and soul, to find out if, indeed, he or she is the right one to marry?

I think there is.

And it has to do with communication: namely, asking good questions and following up with focused listening. Good marriages thrive when couples communicate with each other through the broad spectrum of experiences and emotions, through all the pain, laughter, and stresses of a relationship. Great relationships happen when individuals learn to speak and listen to each other.

If you are considering marriage in the near future, my hope is that this book will help you to ask the right questions before you walk down the aisle. Asking good questions is the key to exploring a future marriage relationship.

The questions you will find in this book have been used by many couples during their courtship or engagement and are ones I have commonly asked in premarital counseling sessions. They are questions that can be asked in privacy, or, sometimes, in the company of others. They are designed to help you learn more about the person you want to marry.

How to Use This Book

No individual will need to ask all the questions in this book. But there are dozens of good questions on a variety of topics that can provoke some in-depth discussion with the one you love. With a little practice, the questions can be asked within the usual patterns of conversation you share with your partner. He or she may not even know that you are asking questions taken from a book. Or, you might opt to use this book as a mutual discussion tool.

See chapter 8 for more creative suggestions.

Regardless of how you decide to use the questions in this book, they are certain to give you the answers you will need to make a wise, well-informed decision about marriage. The more questions you ask, the more you will know about your partner. It's that simple.

While counseling couples before marriage, I have often observed that many bright and intelligent people simply do not know each other very well. Or, at least, they seem unable to articulate good questions and answers for each other. Some couples have areas of life that they have never mutually explored or talked about—even though they have been acquainted for years. Other couples seem lost in a haze of blind love—unable to see obvious flaws and potential stress points that might lead to a breakdown of the marriage. And then, yes, there are those couples who seem to have it all together—who ask the right questions and get honest answers (although not always the ones they want to hear).

Take Calvin and Julie, for instance.

Calvin and Julie were the first couple I ever counseled before marriage. They were both twenty-four years old, had grown up in different towns, gone to different high schools, and had few mutual friends. They had met each other at a favorite bar after a college football game some three or four months before they came to me with a request for marriage.

Since this was my first wedding, and I wanted to do a good and thorough job, naturally I met with them numerous times. We talked about many things: sports, cars, hobbies, a bit of religion, music, movies. But after several hours together it occurred to me that Calvin and Julie were asking all the wrong questions of each other. They had many mutual interests in sports, hobbies, and music. But none of these things seemed capable of supporting a lifetime of marriage. The things we talked about in our counseling sessions were the same things they talked about when they were alone. Few good questions, little substance, no new revelations about each other.

Beginning again, I asked this couple to write out, individually, several questions each would like to ask the other (even if the questions seemed embarrassing or self-serving). Their questions astounded me.

Calvin wanted to ask Julie about some of her bad habits, why she did things that irritated him. He wanted to know more about her family in California. He was uncertain about a relationship she had once shared with a friend of his.

Julie, likewise, had a few good questions of her own. She wanted to ask about Calvin's drinking. She wanted to know more about his younger brother who was mentally retarded. She ventured the uncomfortable question about his seeming obsession with flirtatious younger girls.

As Calvin and Julie asked good questions, their relationship began to change. The answers each provided the other were not always well received or appreciated, but they were honest ones. They began to see each other in a new light. Their relationship grew stronger as a result.

Using the questions in this book may not change your relationship overnight, may not make it better, more loving, or more solid, but the questions will most certainly provide you with information that can help you know your loved one more intimately.

Often, when people think about intimacy in a relationship, they think about sex. But intimacy, by its very definition, has more to do with the depth of a relationship than sexuality. Intimacy has to do with knowledge—the extent to which one knows another person. Intimacy is knowing what makes another person tick—where one hurts, how one is vulnerable, why one laughs, and what makes one cry. This is true intimacy. And even in good, healthy relationships, it is tough to achieve.

Hence the need for frequent questions and discussion, open listening, and the sharing of honest feelings.

If you are considering marriage soon, think about your relationship. Use your own powers of reason. What questions would you ask if you could, if you were not afraid of embarrassment or rejection? What tough questions would help you to get to know your loved one more intimately?

If there are questions that come immediately to mind, chances are you need to sit down and have some heart-to-heart conversations with your partner. You might find just the question in this book that will help you to find the answer you have been seeking. With that answer comes a deeper, more fulfilling and honest relationship.

Before looking through the contents of the book, take a moment to consider a television program that aired back in the 1960s and '70s: *The Dating Game.* I'm sure you remember it or have seen reruns of the show.

On this program, contestants (within a limited amount of time) were allowed to ask questions to a panel of possible dates, all hidden behind a wall. Based upon the answers the contestant received, he/she would then choose a date from among the unseen menagerie.

Even though we know this was just a television program, and that the questions that were asked were often intentionally silly or provocative, there is still much to be learned from it. The show was a study in human behavior and the relationship between the sexes. Some men and women knew how to ask the right questions to get the information they needed to choose "Mister Right" or "Miss Wonderful." And often, simply based upon the answers they received, they were correct in their assessment of their dream date.

Those who could not ask good questions or who balked at giving honest answers (but instead tried to be funny, lewd, or spiteful) often lost out on a chance to meet someone special. And we, the viewers, got to see it all.

While none of us likes to make wrong choices in relationships, we know that there is a greater possibility of doing so when we don't have adequate information about another person. When it comes to considering marriage, the old adages do not apply:

What we don't know won't hurt us.
No news is good news.
Take a chance.
Ask me no questions and I'll tell you no lies.

All of these maxims, if taken to heart in our relationships, will spell certain doom. True love should never be left to chance. We should never play dumb when it comes to knowing more about the person we think we would like to marry.

I hope you will use these questions to deepen your relationship and start you on the road to a loving, fulfilling marriage.

This new edition also comes at a time when social media, Twitter, texting, and new forms of communication are the norm. Younger couples using this book (or a digital copy) may discover that they enjoy talking to each other face-to-face—and that these discussions are opening a new level of intimacy and trust. Embrace this deep place together and continue to open your mind and heart. This is where you will be living out your marriage.

Be mindful, too, that while social media sites like Facebook can provide a forum for communicating with family and friends, they have their downside as well. For example, you may be the type of person who doesn't mind posting photographs of your beach vacation or your children's school accomplishments. Your spouse, on the other hand, may not want your personal life so readily available to strangers. Anything posted online is, after all, "out there"—and it will be out there for a long time.

Couples would do well to discuss their philosophy and approach to using social media—even when it comes to posting wedding and honeymoon photos and commentary—and then be willing to abide by these rules. Many couples today see a breakdown of trust via their use of social media—and we've all heard those stories about people who post their feelings about their jobs, their spouses, and their children only to wake up one morning to discover that they are unemployed, divorced, and estranged from their families. So make sure you have a clear understanding of how you will use social media in your relationship and, more importantly, what you will guard and not release for public consumption.

Keep in mind that we do live in a fast-paced world—and everyone seems to be moving at breakneck speed in work and family. This book—and more importantly your discussions with each other—will provide you with a quiet center where you can discover each other and grow trust and intimacy. Begin practicing good communication techniques while you use this book. Turn off the TV and computer when you are talking to each other. Silence your cell phones. Give each other your full attention. Don't rush. Be open. Be honest.

There are many ways you will communicate with each other in marriage—but let face-to-face talk be the norm. You have much to look forward to—and looking at each other is the place to begin.

Once you begin using this book together, you will also discover that one question might lead to another question that is unrelated—or even not found in this book. Go with your instincts. This book is meant to help you discover each other more fully and communicate effectively by asking good questions. But that doesn't mean you don't have good questions of your own, or that there isn't much to be learned from allowing your conversations to evolve on their own merits. You might have a special time set apart each week to use this book, or you might simply keep the book at hand and use it in conjunction with other conversations you are having.

Solid and clear communication goes well beyond words. Good communication also has to do with how you look at each other, your posture, your response, your listening, and even your silence. Couples who develop solid communication patterns before marriage will deepen their relationship in the years ahead.

CHAPTER ONE

QUESTIONS TO ASK
YOUR FUTURE SPOUSE

*A good marriage is one which allows for change
and growth in the individuals.*
—PEARL S. BUCK

L ife teaches that change is inevitable. The earth constantly moves and shakes; clouds rise and form, spill
and evaporate; plants sprout, take root, and invade the
landscape.

People change, too. This is a fact of life. Any good
relationship acknowledges that individuals do not remain
the same over a period of time. We change in appearance,
outlook, and in our knowledge of the world around us. We
grow emotionally, intellectually, relationally, and spiritually
through time as well.

It has been my observation that, before two people
begin to plan a wedding ceremony, they should first stop
to acknowledge and explore this reality of change. It

surfaces quickly once a man and woman begin sharing the same space, squeezing from the same toothpaste tube, and coming home to mixed piles of dirty clothes. Love shared during courtship may be quite different from the love shared in marriage.

Honoré de Balzac once wrote: "Marriage is a science." In this respect, growing in our understanding of another person could be a form of social science.

In this opening section, you will note that there are fourteen areas of importance that two people should explore before marriage. Try to ask your future spouse questions pertaining to these facets of life, since each of these areas will play a major role in your marital relationship. Marriage is based on mutual love, respect, and trust. The deeper you explore the questions in each of these areas, the greater the possibility that you will be prepared to adapt to the ups and downs of life and the inevitable changes that are heading your way.

The fourteen areas are:

1. Your Hopes and Dreams: Planning a Future Together
2. Family Background and History
3. Education
4. Life Experiences
5. Career
6. Ethics and Values
7. Love and Commitment
8. Sexuality
9. Children/Family

Dinner or Movie?

Obviously, the questions and answers that you and your future spouse share with each other are of greatest importance. As you begin to think about asking some of the questions in this section, consider for a moment the amount of time you actually spend in intimate settings. Are most of your days or evenings spent in the company of others, or do you find time to be alone? Do you spend more time talking over a nice dinner or staring, transfixed, at a movie or television screen? Do you spend more time in the noisy atmosphere of the bowling alley or in the quiet solitude of the living room?

These are good questions to ask yourself before you prepare to ask questions of your future spouse. If you find yourself spending more time in places and settings where intimate conversation is next to impossible, consider first the need to make a quiet space where good conversation can occur. Instead of going to another movie, cook a nice meal together, go to a quiet restaurant, take a walk in the moonlight. Find those peaceful and relaxing moments to pop a few good questions. You will both live to appreciate it.

When two people are in love, good questions and conversation can be a powerful stimulant. As you begin to discuss some of these questions in detail, be assured that the two of you will take each other to places you never dreamed of. As you learn more and more about each other, you will find that your love deepens, your appreciation and trust of the other are strengthened, and your happiness grows.

However, when I counsel couples, sometimes I find that good questions can be a source of anguish and frustration. Some people feel threatened when they are forced to answer intimate questions about their past, their personal tastes and habits, or their dreams for the future. They feel vulnerable opening their hearts to another person—even someone they love. Instead, they prefer to keep their relationship on the surface, never allowing it to deepen.

So you may be asking: What happens if these questions draw us further apart instead of closer together?

My answer to this dilemma is simple: Change and growth are difficult. If your loved one needs to grow up in some areas, or needs to face certain issues head-on, running away from these issues will not deepen your relationship but will instead postpone the inevitable conflicts that are certain to come later in marriage. If you find that your loved one is withholding information and feelings from you now, his/her communication and attitude will not improve after you are married.

Take the time to talk about the difficult subjects now! If you find that your loved one is hesitant to respond to your questions and desire for deeper communication and sharing, be aware that this may be the most revealing development in your relationship. Perhaps your loved one's resistance to communication and exploration is a sign that this person may not be right for you.

Or, if you find that your beloved is merely hesitant and needs a push to get started, try utilizing some of the communication techniques found in the last chapter of this book.

In some instances, as the questions are explored, a person may find that he or she does not wish to continue a relationship. This in itself is not a bad thing. Marriage is built on assurance and certainty. Don't hesitate to put a relationship on hold if you find that your partner is holding back or seems unwilling to communicate or thinks these questions are too personal. Couples in the best marriages have asked all these questions and many more! Better to take it slow now than to dissolve the union in court later.

For this reason, begin by asking questions about your hopes and dreams together. These are positive questions that will get your discussion off to a great start and will help you to face the future with confidence.

Your Hopes and Dreams: Planning a Future Together

Where do you see us living ten years from now?
I'll admit that some people have a difficult time imagining where they will be living *tomorrow*, much less ten *years* from now. But this question will always provoke some serious thought. Søren Kierkegaard, a famous theologian, once said, "We understand life from the past, but we live life for the future." How true.

No doubt, if your loved one can answer the question about where he hopes to be living in ten years, chances are good that he can also tell you *why*. Maybe your dream is to live in a big house in the country. But his dream might be to live in a Manhattan apartment. Either way, you've each said a great deal about where you think your marriage is headed in terms of physical location and lifestyle. Where you hope to live says a great deal about how you hope to get there.

What do you hope I will contribute to our marriage?
This is a very general question, but it can be made specific by adding any of the following ideas: *What do you hope I will contribute in terms of income? What do you want my role to be in the home? In child rearing?*

There is stress in many marriages at the point where the roles are ambiguous. For example, a husband may expect his wife to be the "happy homemaker"—doing all the cooking, cleaning, laundry, child rearing, and such. Likewise, a wife might expect her husband to keep the cars running, mow the lawn, or pay the bills.

Time spent talking about roles within marriage is very important. Throw tradition out the window and focus, instead, upon each other's gifts and talents. You may find that you are the best manager of money. He might handle the laundry like a dream. And you may enjoy doing yard work together.

You might even make some type of simple contract together.

I will do the following: 1. _____ 2. _____ 3. _____ etc.
You will do the following: 1. _____ 2. _____ 3. _____ etc.
We will share these responsibilities: _____
_____
_____

What do you hope you will contribute to our marriage?

Listen to what your loved one says about himself/herself. This will tell you much about his/her initiative, creativity, and care. Consider these contributions and weigh them within the hopes and dreams you are bringing to the marriage.

How do your loved one's contributions align with your own expectations?

What do you hope to be doing when you are forty-five?
This is a good midlife question and can be tailored to your individual circumstances. If you are already in midlife, move the question down the road a bit and ask about retirement.

All of us have hopes and dreams for midlife. Some people hope for financial security by the time they are in their mid-forties. Others want to be able to finance their children's educations. Still others want to have the mortgage retired and all debts paid.

Couples who are able to grow and change together, who are striving for common goals and dreams, have the best marriages. Once mutual goals are established, it is much easier to strive for and obtain them.

Where would you like to retire?
I've spent a good chunk of my life talking to retired people. And, without fail, those who have the most comfortable retirements are the couples who had planned their golden years when they were young.

One retired couple I know (and they are certainly not extravagantly wealthy) have two homes—a summer one in Indiana and a winter one in Florida. Enjoying the sunshine had been their lifelong passion, and now they bask in it year-round.

Financial experts suggest that a couple should begin planning for retirement as soon as they are married. This way, nothing is left to chance.

Before getting married, couples would do well to discuss

their hopes and dreams about their golden years. These types of discussions also have a psychological bonus: those who plan the ending of their lives together are more likely to stay together through the better and worse, the richer and poorer moments of marriage. Or, as the old adage states, "When one is planning a journey, it always helps to know where one is going."

If you had one day left to live, how would you live it?

This is not meant to be a morbid question, but rather a thought-provoking way to help us analyze priorities in life. Priorities are indicative of those things we value most.

I've asked this question in many settings, and most people respond by saying they would spend their last day with the people who are most precious to them. They would want to *live the day to the fullest*, perhaps visit a special place, or tie up a few loose ends that would make life better for the ones they love.

Some people would also try to express their love, their values, and their hopes to others—particularly family and friends.

Thinking about the brevity of life can only serve to strengthen our resolve to make our lives meaningful and productive, especially our relationships with those we love.

What do you do for fun?

During a recent family vacation I noted that bungee jumping now seems to be the activity of choice for many lovers.

Bound together at the ankles and shoulders, couples plunge from great heights to experience the thrill of a lifetime.

Not everyone would consider this fun, but I'm certain that you can manufacture your own good times. Common interests and plenty of laughter go a long way in any marriage. And teaching your individual interests to your beloved can be an excellent opportunity to bond even more.

How often do you like to have time to yourself?

I have always been a person who likes and needs to spend large chunks of time alone. Beginning in grade school, I found that these solitary times were most important to my general state of mind and happiness. However, my wife enjoys socializing and cavorting with others as often as possible. At times this has been a conflict in our relationship. So, we have to work on this aspect of our marriage. I have to give up more of my solitude; she has to sacrifice more of her social times.

Be aware that some people are energized by solitude and drained by interaction. Others are energized by interaction and bored with solitude. Work together to reach a common understanding and appreciation of each other's needs.

How often do you like to get together with your friends?

Everyone brings his/her own friendships and past relationships into a marriage: people we have known since high school, college pals, friends made in the workplace or at social events. Marriage is never lived in a vacuum.

So it will be only natural that you and your fiancé will want to continue these relationships in some fashion. Talking about these friendships will heighten your awareness of the broad spectrum of people who have made a difference in your lives. By making plans to meet some of these friends before the wedding, each of you might gain a few new friends in the process. Perhaps you could organize a few parties or host one or two gatherings that would enable you to meet each other's friends.

Great friendships add so much to a good marriage and give you a network of support.

Where would you like to live immediately after the wedding? Why?

This question might provoke an entire discussion about your future together. Where you choose to live will be one of the most important facets of your marriage relationship, since it touches upon everything from career choices, to housing, to where your children will go to school.

Given the fact that we are such a transient society, moving from place to place quickly is no longer much of a problem in the physical sense. But moving does take an emotional toll and can be a source of tension in a marriage.

Talk about your reasons for wanting to live in a certain city, state, or area of the country. Try to weigh all the pluses and minuses in a fair and cooperative fashion to arrive at a decision that will benefit you both.

How close do you want to live to your parents?

For many people, proximity to one's parents has little value. For others, this issue may have great emotional attachment. Likewise, some people may feel a need to be close to parents who are aging, or who have physical or financial needs. All these concerns should be talked about in an open and honest manner.

If you are going to be living close to parents, consider the following questions: How will I like seeing his/her/my parents frequently? Will his/her/my parents give me the space and independence I desire in my marriage? How will living close to parents affect my parenting style?

If you are going to be living far away from parents, consider these questions: How will distance affect my/our relationship with parents? Will I/we like having to travel a distance to see family? How often will we try to see his/her/my parents?

Will you want to change your name after marriage?

It is still the case that, for many women in society, a change of name accompanies marriage. But this tradition has changed over the years. Now, many women prefer to keep their "maiden" name or, perhaps, use a hyphenated combination of maiden and married names.

In my counseling sessions I have found that many couples have not considered or discussed this issue before marriage. Or, perhaps, they have not yet arrived at a mutual decision.

One couple I know chose a unique alternative. They

both changed their last names, taking a surname from a Hebrew word, *Ruach*, which means "breath" or "spirit."

The names you both choose will have implications for your children. Any changes made will also be legally binding. Both of you will want to feel good about the decision, since you will be using your names for life. For this reason you should think carefully about this issue before completing the marriage license. The informed decisions you make before the wedding will assure that you will not be misaddressed later.

Which holidays hold special importance for you? Why? Which holidays will we spend with which family?

The celebration and sharing of holidays is an important traditional element in every marriage. No doubt each of you will bring your own memories, hopes, and wishes to bear upon these special times.

Because holidays are, by definition, sacred and laden with strong feelings, I encourage couples to give careful consideration to how they will celebrate these times in their marriage. Some couples will attempt to make the most of every holiday, traveling back and forth from various points in order to spend time with each family. Others make the decision to establish their own tradition or may opt to take turns with the various holidays, seeing his family one year and hers the next. No doubt, as children come into the picture, even these traditions and desires will change.

Couples who bring differing religious traditions to a

marriage will find an added pressure—juggling twice as many holidays, diets, and customs. But good communication and planning can go a long way toward alleviating any problems.

Couples who reach an understanding about holidays before the wedding day will find their holidays to be less stressful and confrontational. If at all possible, try to commit your yearly itinerary to paper so that certain family members do not get ignored or left out.

Family Background and History

None of us experiences life in a vacuum. We live in relation to others and recall life as a narrative, a tapestry of stories, events, and people who have shaped us and made us who we are.

For this reason, exploring your background and history with your fiancé will be an important aspect of your life together. For example, if you know the major events and moments in your sweetheart's life, then you will have greater insight and appreciation of the attitudes and opinions he/she shares. You will know why your loved one has certain fears, certain dislikes, or needs certain types of affirmation. Perhaps your loved one grew up in a home with an alcoholic father or was once mugged. Knowing this history might help explain why your fiancé seems uncomfortable in bars or has a pathological fear of ski masks. Without this history to draw upon, your relationship would be one-dimensional, having no depth or foundation upon which to build your lives together.

Here you will find questions to help you and your fiancé explore your childhood experiences, families, and backgrounds.

How would you describe your childhood?

Psychologists and sociologists tell us that most of our adult patterns of behavior, fears, and personality traits are formed within the first years of childhood. Therefore, it stands to reason that our childhood environments have much to tell us about each other.

When counseling couples, I always spend a sizeable portion of time asking about their childhood and adolescent years. All of us carry emotional scars and subconscious baggage from our childhoods. On the one hand, we may feel hurt, victimized, neglected, angry, or ignored.

On the other hand, we may have also experienced warmth, expressions of love, support, and touches that upheld us in moments of despair. We bring these same expectations and desires for warmth to our marriage.

Talking about our childhoods is one of the best ways to gain a greater understanding of another person. And, since we remember in narrative, most of our childhood recollections have become stories—events now somewhat larger than life that have helped to define us. Ask this question, and I think you will find the stories cannot be exhausted in one sitting. Our memories are a deep well, and they tell us much about where we have come from, how we are likely to behave and feel, and why we have established certain patterns and habits in our lives.

How did your parents treat you?
How well did you get along with your parents?

There's a rule I like to pass on to couples contemplating marriage: A man looks for a woman who reminds him of his mother (nurturing, caring, loving); a woman looks for a man who reminds her of her father (supportive, dependable, strong). There are exceptions, of course. But the pattern usually holds true.

And there is another rule: A woman should observe how her fiancé treats his own mother. This is how she can expect to be treated. A man should observe how his fiancée relates to her own father. This is how he can expect to be treated.

Some of the most uncomfortable weddings I have ever conducted featured brides who could not get along with their own fathers and grooms who continually berated their own mothers during the rehearsal and on the day of the ceremony. I fear for such couples, knowing that this is probably the way they are going to relate to each other.

What is the happiest memory of your childhood?

During the years I was growing up, I knew my father was a hard worker. He left for work early in the morning (including Saturdays) and arrived home as my mother was setting the supper table. But he would always have enough energy to play a game of basketball with me each night (a religious ritual in Indiana, where basketball is a divine right).

Imagine my joy and surprise when, upon returning home from school one day, I found that my father had spent the entire day creating a basketball court in our yard, complete with new goal and ball. I knew how much time and energy he had dedicated to the task. It meant a lot. Over the years, we had many special games on that basketball court, and more than a few father and son talks.

Everyone should be blessed with such wonderful memories of childhood.

How would you describe your relationship with your brothers and sisters?

Sibling rivalry doesn't always end when we graduate from high school. In some families, it's like an open sore. I always have to shake my head when I see this rivalry oozing out on the day of a wedding when everyone should be concentrating on the joy of the newly married couple.

Everyone entering into a marriage should be mature enough to say something about the relationship shared with his or her siblings. It always helps to have a supportive extended family to lean on from time to time. And most families do manage this kind of love.

But if your partner has strained relationships with certain brothers or sisters, please take note of this and make adjustments accordingly. You may not always be able to avoid family gatherings and reunions, but you can certainly help your husband or wife avoid the undue stress of having to deal with a brother or sister who is a constant source of irritation.

How was love expressed in your home when you were growing up?

We have all experienced love in different ways. Some of us grew up in homes where love was not only expressed verbally but also demonstrated with lots of hugs and kisses. Others of us grew up in a loving environment but perhaps did not receive verbal or physical expressions of affection. In essence, we have all experienced touch in different ways. We have heard love expressed in different fashions. And we learned to return love in our own styles.

Talking about your history of touch can be a key element in any future relationship. For example, some men are natural huggers; others are not. If a woman expects not only verbal expressions of love but also fond caresses and hugs, she should understand that these expressions may not come easily for some men. Likewise, some men long for daily kisses but may not always find a willing partner.

How did your parents express their love for you?
How often were you held or caressed by your parents?
Can you think of a time when you were most aware of your parents' love?

If you want to deepen your discussion about family background and history, ask one or two of these questions. You will be certain to gain some new understandings and insights about your loved one's history of expressing affection, and how these experiences and expectations will become a part of your marriage.

How would you describe your current relationship with your parents?

This is a good question to ask if you have yet to meet your loved one's parents. Because we live in a very transient society, families are much less connected than they used to be. Some sons and daughters live hundreds, even thousands, of miles apart from their parents. And there are occasions when a bride or groom might meet the new in-laws for the first time at the wedding.

Give your future spouse an opportunity to describe his parents and the kind of relationship they share.

Do you or your family have a history of any diseases or medical conditions?

This may seem an awkward question, but it has some practical applications. Medical science is learning more every day about congenital defects and predispositions related to cancer, heart disease, and even mental illness. Some people, genetically, are at greater risk than others.

Now, you will probably not break off an engagement if you discover that all the males in your loved one's family have died of heart attacks, but this knowledge will certainly let you know what you might expect in the way of future health concerns. Some congenital predispositions might also be a concern for you if you plan to have children. So it is best to know the health history of the person you are going to marry.

If you suspect that there are going to be serious health concerns for the two of you, I would advise that you consult a physician and give a breakdown of your medical conditions and histories. A doctor might be able to recommend precautions, diets, or medications that could help.

In this age of AIDS and other incurable viruses, you will want to make certain that your future partner is open about his or her medical history. Talking about health issues might also lead you into discussions about your partner's sexual history, addictions (such as drug or alcohol abuse), or bad habits (such as smoking). Certainly you will want to know all you can about the health and well-being of the one you are going to marry.

How did/does your family deal with anger and confrontation?

Anger is a healthy and needed emotion, and is a reality in every marriage. Sooner or later, when the honeymoon is over, anger, resentment, and confrontations seep into every relationship. That's a part of life.

Anger that is dealt with, talked about, and resolved is healthy and stabilizing in a marriage. But when anger goes unexpressed, is ignored, or becomes unchecked in physical or verbal torrents of abuse, the very fabric of love can be destroyed.

Discovering how your loved one's family deals with anger is one key in understanding how he/she will likely treat you when there is a conflict. As a pastor, I have seen firsthand the vicious cycle of abuse (not always the physical variety) that can tear marriages apart. Those who were abused as children, or witnessed abuse in the home, often grow up to abuse their own spouses and children.

If your fiancé/fiancée is open about his/her family background, you might even learn some new techniques for resolving conflict in your own marriage. Many couples have learned how to have a good argument, reach resolution, and then go to bed as friends before the lights are turned out at night. This type of peaceful resolution and marital tranquillity is something every marriage should strive for.

Was there a lot of confrontation in your family? If yes, what about?

Some years back I met with a young married couple who could not seem to resolve certain conflicts in their relationship. After a mere three months, their marriage had gone from wonderful to dreadful. The primary reason for this downward spiral was their inability to deal with confrontation in a healthy manner.

He had grown up in a home where there was much confrontation—usually centering on money, or the lack of it. But these conflicts were never resolved without much shouting and bickering on the part of his parents and siblings. She, on the other hand, had grown up in a home where conflicts were settled by a stern and forceful father. His word and will were considered inviolable.

With these two histories bearing upon their marriage, it was not surprising that this young couple was unable to resolve their conflicts. He wanted to settle confrontations through mutual bantering and shouting—an emotional battle of give and take. But she wanted an authoritative word, which was no longer there.

As you and your loved one explore family confrontations from the past, you will learn much about what you need to do to resolve your own conflicts when they arise. You might expect some of the same confrontations to crop up in your marriage from time to time. Talk about it now, and try to reach a consensus as to how you will handle conflict in the future.

What do you consider your mother's worst trait?
What do you consider your mother's best trait?
Very few of us want to speak ill of our mother . . . and we have equal difficulty speaking of their strengths. On the one hand, if we speak of our mothers' weaknesses, we feel that we are somehow betraying the one who nurtured us from the womb. And if we speak of her strengths, we are somehow heaping praise upon ourselves. ("I am living proof of my mother's genius!")

In spite of these difficulties, however, you deserve to know how your fiancé/fiancée understands and appreciates his/her mother. Mothers are the most difficult species on earth to comprehend and analyze, and yet they give us so much. At times mothers are overbearing and overprotective—at other times so freeing and supportive.

It has been said that a woman can gauge a man's love and good intentions by the way he treats and talks about his mother. I've come to believe that there is much truth in that notion.

What do you consider your father's worst trait?
What do you consider your father's best trait?

Once you have asked about your fiancé's mother, why not ask a few questions about Dad?

I know I have always appreciated the many small sacrifices my father made for me when I was growing up. I saw evidence of this each day. But many of my friends were not so fortunate. Sometimes their fathers were absent or abusive or negligent in their nurture and care. So I know that when the word *father* is spoken, not everyone has a positive image.

Talking about your parents is one way for the two of you to grow closer together. The deeper your knowledge of your fiancé's history, the stronger your bridge will be to the future.

How did your parents show affection for each other?

It has been said that the greatest gift we can give to our children is a good marriage. If you grew up in a home where your parents' affection for each other was apparent, chances are you have sought out a partner who can show you that same degree of love.

Nevertheless, it is helpful to find out how your fiancé noticed these signs of affection. Your question might inspire him/her to appreciate a warm and loving family.

How were you disciplined as a child?

As a parent, I know that discipline is an uncertain science. There are times when I have felt the need to be stern and unyielding in my expectations (and have even expressed anger toward my son and daughter). And there have been times when I have experimented with a variety of sly psychological ploys—all attempts (usually vain ones) to force my children to conform to some principle or guideline my wife or I had established.

I suppose I continue these patterns of discipline with my children because these were the same methods my parents used on me.

You and your fiancé may discover that you were disciplined in different ways as children. Perhaps you grew up in a home where spanking or "going without supper" were standard discipline fare. But your fiancé may have grown up in a home where these methods were never used.

Discussing this aspect of your histories might help you to talk about your hopes for children or, perhaps, how best to discipline children when you begin the awesome task of parenting.

Did you feel listened to as a child?
Did you feel secure as a child?
Since so many of our personal habits and patterns of behavior are established early in life, it stands to reason that you will want to know as much as possible about your loved one's childhood. Often, when I meet with couples, I find that they enjoy talking about childhood memories and feelings. Perhaps this is just a sense of nostalgia, but couples also have a genuine desire to understand each other's past.

Many of the patterns and good feelings we enjoyed as children will carry over into our adult lives.

When you were a child, what did you want to be when you grew up?
Our childhood hopes and dreams had an important place in shaping our first efforts and goals. Through desire, we learn how to focus our powers of intellect upon achieving the dream. These early hopes help to shape our self-confidence and esteem.

Reality dictates that some people achieve their dreams and others do not. Some doors open and others close. We realize as adults that we do not get everything we desire in life.

It is fascinating to talk about how our early goals took shape, how they changed through time, and what we have learned about ourselves in the process.

Education

This section on education encompasses not only past experiences and education history but also the aspirations that you and your fiancé may share about continued learning—formal or otherwise. These questions will help you to work out your dreams, and will set you on a road to planning and success.

You will want to know something about the educational background of the one you are going to marry. Regardless of whether your future spouse attended high school or a university, a trade school or technical college, you will want to explore your different educational backgrounds. Discussing your various histories of education will help you to find common qualities and interests you can share for a lifetime.

What educational experiences have helped shape your life?

No two people learn in the same way. Some of us are auditory learners: we access and store new information best when we can hear it. Others of us learn through visual concepts and approaches—blackboards, books, or charts. Still others learn best through firsthand experiences, such as fieldwork and on-the-job training.

Educational experiences need not be limited to a formal school setting but can take a variety of avenues. Life itself is a learning experience, and I have known many people who, although having little formal education, have impressed me with their great wisdom and insights.

Attempt to make your marriage itself a learning and growing experience—intellectually. Challenge each other to continue seeking, asking, and learning. Never give up your quest for new knowledge and understanding of the vast world around us. Try to make your future spouse a better person by giving him/her new educational experiences.

When you were in school, what studies did you most enjoy?
What was your college major?

Again, common interests go a long way in any relationship. If you have an interest in science or computer technology, you will enjoy spending time with a spouse who shares these same interests.

College educations have changed over the years. I find that many people today do not major in the subject they most enjoy studying. Today job placement and financial concerns are often at the forefront of educational decisions. Many people want to earn a degree in an area that will give them an edge, that will open doors of opportunity in new and expanding frontiers which will pay well or provide future security. I see nothing wrong with this, but I know that many people do have other interests outside of their areas of training. So it might serve you well to talk about those areas of study that were not reflected in your major. You may discover some new intellectual bonding.

Do you see yourself ever going back to school?

Continuing education is a necessity in many occupations. New technologies, inventions, and methodologies force many people back into the classroom. Likewise, many people with high school degrees are opting, sometimes after decades in the workforce, to go back to school to earn a college degree. Changes in the workplace, the shifting world market, and expanding overseas investments will make education all the more necessary in the future. Other people enjoy exploring their fields or outside interests in the classroom, regardless of the financial return. They enjoy a university setting and cherish new knowledge and insights.

If you or your fiancé is considering going back to school at some point, why not discuss the particulars?

What is he/she hoping to study?

When might he/she go back to school?

What are the advantages and disadvantages to this decision and how will it affect your marriage?

What kind of experiences did you have in school (elementary grades, high school, college, graduate school)? Did you like school?

The years we spend in school are not reserved exclusively for academics. During our school years we learn how to develop friendships, how to compete in sports, and how to organize our lives. We learn to define ourselves and establish our values as we come into contact with others.

Everyone has experiences that have helped to shape their aspirations and understandings of life. Couples who talk about these experiences not only learn more about each other but also come to appreciate their own friendships and memories.

Did you make many friends throughout your years in school?
Are you still in contact with any of these friends?

The years we spend in school are some of the most traumatic and challenging of our lives. Particularly in grade school and high school, our friendships helped to define us and enabled us to develop the emotional and intellectual "tools" needed in adulthood. With our friends we dreamed about the future, shared wonderful times of laughter and joy, and overcame great hardships and difficulties. It is only natural that these early friendships will mean something to us.

If you and your fiancée attended different schools, try using a high school or college yearbook as you talk about these friends. No doubt you will want to invite some of these friends to your wedding, so it is especially helpful to see their names and faces.

How important is education to you? College?

Not many years ago I entertained the notion of going back to college to work on a Ph.D. This would have been a major decision for me—and my wife—as we already had children, careers, and a degree of security. We talked about this decision, and what it would mean to us (and what we would have to give up), and finally decided that the timing was not right.

Since that time, my wife has talked about returning to college as well. Education (or, in our case, furthering our education) has always been important to us. But there are always many aspects of such a decision to consider—including cost, time, and other commitments.

The older I get, the more I realize how often my formal education needs to be updated in light of new knowledge, technological advances, and the ever-changing world. Even if one doesn't have a college degree, or has no plans to pursue such an education, that is no reason to quit learning. Education is a lifetime achievement. Learning never ceases. By talking about your future educational plans with each other, the two of you can begin to plot a course of continued learning that can add new dimensions to every aspect of your marriage.

How would you describe your leaning style?

Some people are visual learners; others are auditory. Likewise, some people prefer taking online courses to classroom sessions. Your spouse's learning style will also be important to your communication methods, and with the advent of so much information online and through web-based learning, every couple would do well to discuss how their learning styles are similar or different.

Life Experiences

As far as we know, human beings are the only creatures on earth who can draw from their wealth of memories. Each one of us makes daily decisions based upon what we have learned from the past. If we park our car in a tow-away zone and return later to find that the car has been towed, we will not be likely to park there again. Likewise, when we learn that saying "I love you" makes someone feel good, we understand that we have the power to build someone up in a special way. We are, in essence, composed of life experiences. We define ourselves by recalling where we have come from, whom we have known, and the places we have been.

As you explore life experiences with your fiancé, I trust that you will listen carefully, not so much to the words, as the feelings behind them. Allow these questions to help you become more knowledgeable of the person you love.

What is your greatest accomplishment or triumph?

I believe that everyone has something in his/her life that can be considered a great accomplishment.

I know people who have overcome enormous hardships to gain a college education. I have some good friends who literally went from rags to riches in a matter of a few years—all because of a triumph in a business venture.

There are others who deserve top grades for their parenting skills, their involvement in charitable organizations, or their leadership in the community.

You and your fiancé also have much to celebrate in this regard. Each of you has a great achievement that should be recognized and commended by the other.

If you could change one event in your past, what would it be?

A few years ago I attended a retirement dinner in honor of a prominent community leader. After this esteemed leader delivered his moving speech, one line of his talk lingered in my mind: "I retire today having lived a life of no regrets."

No regrets? That one line changed my entire perception of the man. How, I wondered, was it possible for a person to live without regrets? It seems to me that a life without regrets is a shallow and unexamined life.

I know that in the course of my life I have made many bad choices. There are things I wish I could do over again. If I knew then what I know now, I could have done them better. There are roads that, in retrospect, now look more enticing than the paths I have chosen. I wish I had loved more, given more, taken more risks in my youth.

When you begin to find out more about the one you love, you will inevitably learn of the disappointments in that person's life. Sharing our lost dreams is the first step in making a few others come true.

What is the greatest lesson you've learned in life?

In marriage, life experiences can teach us as much as any formal education. Some of us have learned how to be good stewards of money, not by taking accounting classes but by managing an allowance when we were young. Others of us have a natural way of relating to people, which is a skill not taught in any university.

Anyone who is a student of life will certainly have an experience or two to share. If you find that your loved one hasn't learned anything in life, you might want to ask yourself, "Will he/she learn anything in our marriage?"

How much have you traveled?

It is a rare individual these days who has not traveled beyond the bounds of his/her home state. Going to new places, seeing new things, meeting new people—all these are important life experiences that help us to grow and mature in our understanding of the world and other people. *National Geographic* is wonderful, but nothing compares to seeing the beauty and splendor of an actual place.

Chances are, if you have been to Paris, you will want to show your photos and video to your fiancé. Such an adventure will bring up more memories and spark conversation. People who travel a great deal seem to have an outlook on the world quite different from that of those who stay close to home. You will likely want to talk about some of your common experiences and observations about the world we live in. Where a person has been often says much about who he/she is.

Who has been a role model for you, and why?

Everyone is influenced by somebody. This is evidence that none of us passes through life alone, without the assistance and kindness of others.

Perhaps your fiancé has followed the advice and tutelage of someone special. Knowing more about this role model might give you a greater appreciation of his/her gifts and talents, as well as desires in life.

What was your most embarrassing moment?

Okay, so this sounds like a question you probably asked at a junior high slumber party. Nevertheless, it's good to know if the one you love has an ability to laugh at himself/herself. A sense of humor is one of the most important ingredients in a successful marriage.

One couple I know had their most embarrassing moment *together*—at the wedding ceremony! I was officiating at the outdoor wedding, a beautiful poolside affair in the heat of August. Despite the fact that the bride had invited only a handful of close friends and family, she was extremely nervous. Her anxiety, compounded by the fact that she was wearing a full-length bridal gown in such scorching heat, caused her to visibly shake and her makeup to run like jelly. By the time we got to the vows, her face was a rich mixture of colors, and the groom was laughing so hard that he nearly fell into the pool.

Moments later, when I asked for the wedding rings, I noted that the bride appeared a bit flushed. As the best man reached over to hand me the rings, the bride fainted dead away onto the concrete. The groom quickly picked her up, the best man rushed for a bucket of swimming pool water, and the maid of honor ran into the house to fetch some smelling salts.

By the time the bride came to, everyone had forgotten about the rings, but I managed to restore order and we tried a second time. Again the bride fainted. Procedures were repeated. The soggy bride was then propped up in a lawn chair. From this vantage point she managed to repeat her ring vow, gave another gasp, and then collapsed a final time.

A half hour later, with the couple lying next to each other on a four-poster bed, I announced that they were husband and wife, said a final blessing, and then got out of there. Driving away, I couldn't help but feel that, with such a rough beginning, the couple was destined to have a long, smooth life together.

What was the saddest moment of your life?
I always get a lump in my throat when, during the wedding ceremony, I ask the couple to repeat the words: "For better, for worse, for richer, for poorer, in sickness, and in health." I suppose this is because I realize that every marriage will be filled with these inevitable ups and downs of life.

Sadness is as much a necessary component of existence

as are happiness and joy. But I know that, when I talk about my own moments of grief, I am somehow lifted beyond them and experience the healing I need. As two people consider marriage, they would do well to talk about their times of grief. This makes for a much deeper marriage and enables husband and wife to give empathy and support when needed.

Do you have any health issues or concerns that could impact our marriage?

Increasingly, concerns about health care and health-related issues are impacting marriages. Many marital stresses center on money—and health-related costs are now a prime source of many of these difficulties.

It is safe to say that health insurance and health-related costs will deeply impact most marriages—and so talking about these issues up front will be important. Are there health-related concerns that either of you have?

As you discuss these issues, be open about how you feel about diet, regular exercise, obesity, smoking, drinking, and any chronic illnesses or past injuries that may impact your future. Any health-related concern can be addressed—and there is no illness that a couple can't work on together. But begin with honesty. Remember, your mental and emotional health will be just as important as the physical. And good health begins when we love and trust.

What activities motivate you and keep you healthy?
There are many ways to stay fit, to keep our minds active and engaged. Not everyone will want to run a marathon or compete in an iron-man competition. Some people enjoy more cerebral, quiet pastimes. The important aspect of this question is motivation—understanding those activities that keep us alive and bring us joy. Be sure you understand these things about your partner.

Then, talk about some of these activities that you can enjoy together—regardless of whether it's hiking, kayaking, or working crossword puzzles. Motivate each other to eat healthy, live healthy, and work healthy. In the long run your marriage will be more fulfilling and enjoyable if you do some activities together. By pushing each other in healthy ways, you'll discover that the benefits go far beyond your bank account.

What is the best thing that has ever happened to you?
What are some of the high points of your life?
What are you most proud of doing in life?
Life has an odd way of rolling us from one extreme to another. But by talking about some of the high points of life you can gain a greater appreciation of your loved one and share a few laughs. You will gain new respect for your sweetheart's moments of triumph and success.

Life is a series of experiences that can build us up or tear us down. But when you learn to concentrate on the best things of life, even the bad times seem, somehow, endurable. Exploring these pinnacles of life can also be the starting point for many of your future hopes and dreams together.

Also, when we take pride in what we do, there is an energy and happiness that carries over into other facets of life, including marriage. Seek to repeat these moments and you will be assured of much future joy.

Career

An individual's work is one of the most personal human expressions.

Think of it. We spend an enormous number of hours at work. We put a great deal of ourselves into what we do. We take pride in what we accomplish. As such, a career is far more than a job.

The careers that you and your future spouse have chosen will also play a huge role in your family life: the amount of time you will spend together, the level of lifestyle you will have, the amount of vacation and free time you will share together. Career choices will make a difference in your income level, your friendships, and the way each of you feels about the day-to-day affairs of life.

The questions in this section are meant to challenge and deepen your discussion of work-related experiences and goals.

What personal goals do you have in your profession?

Not long ago I married a couple whose marriage ended with a quick divorce two months later. The reason? The fellow had assumed that, once married and receiving the benefit of his wife's higher-paying salary, he could quit his nine-to-five job at the bank and try to start his own wood-widget factory in the garage. His wife had no idea he was into woodworking, but she got in a few good lumps with her lawyer once the chips started to fly.

Talking about your work with your future spouse is extremely important. If a career shift is in order, or one or both of you need to make a move, it is best to get it on the table early so there are no surprises. Your partner's professional goals will be an important aspect of your future together.

Since most of our waking hours are spent at work, it is wise to discuss every aspect of our career plans with the one we love.

How much do you expect to earn over the next five years?

While marriage is not principally about wealth and possessions, it certainly is true that each person brings his/her own financial expectations to bear upon the union. For some people, money is a touchy subject. Some men, for example, are threatened by the possibility (or reality!) that their spouses might earn more than they. But more and more often I'm meeting men who can say with conviction: "I'd love for my wife to make more money than I do!"

Most people want to know how much their spouses can expect to earn in the near future. Knowing the earning power of an individual also helps to alleviate some forms of marital suffering, such as overextended charge cards, empty savings accounts, and bankruptcy courts. Experience has shown me that separate bank accounts are coming back into style in many marriages—with "his" and "hers" allotments.

The sooner you and your spouse can set a budget, the more secure you will feel once the bills start rolling in.

What types of jobs have you had?

A recent study of occupations in America has revealed that most people will work at a variety of jobs during their lifetimes. A generation ago, most people began work at a company and stayed until retirement. Today, it is a rare individual who does not change companies or careers at some point. In fact, fewer than 50 percent of college graduates end up working in the fields for which they studied in college.

Knowing about your loved one's job history will be important as you move into the twenty-first century. People who have a variety of skills and abilities will have a distinct advantage over those who are less flexible. Given the fact that you and your future spouse will most likely change careers or move to a different city, or one or both of you may experience a job layoff at some point, it will be important to understand the strengths, abilities, and flexibility each of you brings to the marriage.

How important is work to you?

A friend of mine was recently laid off from work but surprised me with his good-natured philosophy. "I'm not what I do," he told me. "I'm more than just a job. My work does not define who I am."

The nature and place of work hold different importance to different people. Some people see work as a means to an end—putting bread on the table, raising a family, earning enough to enjoy hobbies and leisure. Others see work as an end in itself—climbing the corporate ladder, earning advancement, working the long hours that will lead to recognition and financial success. There is no right or wrong in either philosophy—just different perspectives on what is important to the individual.

As you and your fiancé talk about your careers, try to weigh the importance of your work against the other aspects of your marriage. Attempt to balance your jobs against the other needs of your relationship. Understanding these differences will help you to resolve conflicts that may arise concerning advancement, long work hours, and the amount of time spent at home.

How many hours a week do you anticipate working?

Every job has its pressures and time demands; some people can work far longer hours than others without feeling burned out.

By discussing the time demands inherent in your work, you and your fiancé will be able to plan more time for each other. Once you have an idea of how many days a week and how many hours a day your work will require, take a look at these additional questions and use them to make the first year of your marriage more enjoyable.

- What day(s) of the week will we take off?
- How can we save time for each other every week?
- How many weeks of vacation do we receive each year?
- From time to time, will we be able to meet each other during the day?
- What will we do if our work schedules conflict with our time together?

Can you forget about your work when you are at home?

For a long time I had difficulty separating my work from my home life. I would often continue working while I was watching television in the evening, or while eating dinner. Eventually this type of schedule and intensity caught up with me. I found that I was irritable and resentful. My family noticed it, too.

The ability to drop the demands and stresses of work when you come home at night is a marvelous gift. Everyone needs downtime each day, especially if one works in a high-activity environment.

When you ask this question, keep in mind that the two of you have made a decision to spend time with each other because of your love. Is there a better reason to get married?

Don't let your work consume the time you need together during the first crucial year of marriage.

Will you be able to work out of the home?

With the advent of personal computers, the Internet, and fax machines, many people are finding that they can work effectively out of their homes. In fact, there are some companies that encourage their employees to work at home. Comfortable and familiar surroundings often make business less stressful and more congenial.

Perhaps you or your fiancé can make this type of an arrangement work in your marriage. Some couples have found that working out of the home is preferable to driving to work on a daily basis. Others have found home employment a viable option when starting a small business or when making a transition to another company. Some couples even work together.

Talk about whether this option is a possibility in each of your lines of work and whether such an arrangement would be helpful or detrimental to your careers and marriage.

Is your work valued by others?
Do you value your work?

Occasionally I counsel people (usually men) who find no value and meaning in their work. They are searching for an occupation that will give their lives a sense of purpose.

Mostly, they want to know that their work is making a difference to someone else.

Perhaps the search for meaning is one of the struggles of modem life. Everyone has a need to feel appreciated and respected, valued by his or her peers, and supported by the leaders of the organization he or she is working for. Some people can find value in work that pays little but reaps large emotional rewards. Other people find value only in a large paycheck, regardless of the stresses they encounter day in and day out.

How good does your loved one feel about his/her work? Does he/she enjoy the challenges? Does he/she feel bored and underappreciated? Do others applaud and compliment his/her work?

These questions are important to you both as you seek to find happiness in what you do.

Are you well liked at work?

During funerals, I like to remind people that at the end of our lives what each of us longs to have said about us is: "He was a good man. She was a good woman." We want to be remembered for good; we want to be well liked; we want other people to respect us and enjoy our company.

A work environment is often a difficult arena in which to get to know people. Sometimes it is difficult to please others. But, in spite of these challenges, good people are still respected and appreciated. Being well liked at work is, perhaps, one of the greatest indicators of integrity and self-assurance. If a person is loved at work, no doubt he/she will be loved by a great many people.

Ethics and Values

Marriage can be a communion of hearts and minds . . . if the two share the same values and are molded by the same ethics.

Be intentional about discussing your values. You and your fiancé will be faced with many challenges in your marriage, and in many instances, you will have to rely upon your higher ideals of faithfulness, truth, and goodness to see you through. If you find that you and your fiancé share many of the same values, you will possess a greater peace and happiness in the years to come.

What do you cherish most in life?

My children fascinate me. One minute my daughter will be playing with a favorite doll, and the next minute she will toss it aside to play with something else. Likewise, my son may favor one toy truck for a day or two, but then, when the newness wears off, he will forget about it for days on end.

My observations have taught me that some adults live

in much the same way. They live by whims and fancies, with no clear certainty of the things they cherish most.

I believe, however, that everyone has the capacity to love and to express warmth. Everyone cherishes something, or somebody. If I were getting married again, I would want to know that my life mate was able to express her love for me and felt comfortable in doing so. Before you get married, attempt to ascertain those qualities that you cherish most in your loved one, and make certain you will not be that one thing which is tossed aside when something more attractive comes along.

How would you describe your values and morals?

Generally I find that people are attracted to others of like-minded character and values. I have yet to meet a bride and groom who are at polar opposites in regard to their philosophies of life, moral conduct, and notions of right and wrong. I have, however, married couples who were of different political persuasions, different faiths, different races, and different nationalities. But in spite of these differences, these couples each maintained a common bond of values and morals.

Marriage is built on trust, love, and commitment.

Couples who share common values are more likely to pull together through the tough times, and will be able to support each other through the challenges and difficulties that test their strength and character. When a husband and wife mutually respect each other's values, the bond of love grows stronger with the passing years.

What gives your life meaning?

Rummaging through the bookstore one day, I ran across a book entitled *The Search for Meaning*. The title caused me to stop and reflect upon that quest.

Of course we all search for meaning. One person finds meaning in a cold beer—another in a cup of tea. One person finds meaning in scaling a dangerous mountain—another in basking in the sanctuary of a warm beach. One person finds meaning in friendship—another in solitude.

Meaning is not always apparent. And that is why we need to ask the question, to get an answer.

In my line of work, I meet many people who are still trying to find the meaning of life. They often assume that meaning is to be found in some distant place or time, or in some mystical experience, or even by adhering to some prescribed set of rules. But for most people, meaning comes in the everyday affairs of life—through our work, our love, our friendships, our marriage. These intangible blessings are worth far more than we can say. Knowing what is meaningful to your partner helps you assist him/her on his/her quest for meaning in his/her life.

Do you have any secrets you would like to tell me?

This is not necessarily a values question, but I like to give couples an opportunity to disclose any long-kept secrets that they may be withholding from each other. Secrets are not necessarily bad things. And the trust of other people should certainly be honored and kept, so don't feel compelled to share confidences you've sworn not to disclose.

But some couples need to share the secrets that may cause a lapse of trust further down the road in marriage. For example, some men might open up and admit that they once made a bad decision with another woman that resulted in a pregnancy. Some women might tell about a lapse of faithfulness while still in the current relationship. I once married a couple in which the groom had disclosed to his fiancée that he had killed his father in self-defense when he was a teenager.

And not all secrets are heavy ones. One fellow admitted that he had never liked his fiancée's hairstyle. One young woman revealed that she felt uncomfortable with his friends. A relationship that can open up to this level of honesty and trust is bound to deepen.

Who are the important people in your life, and what roles do they play?

Before you ask this question, take the time to reflect upon the important people in *your* life. Make a list of people who have influenced you, nurtured you, taught you. Include not only your family and significant friends but also your teachers, coaches, neighbors, and leaders who have made a difference in your life. You will discover that your journey has been shaped and guided by a host of people.

When you consider your own history, you will find that people have passed in and out of your life at various stages of your learning and growth. Perhaps you had a favorite teacher or coach in grade school, someone who influenced you greatly at that time. But now you have new friends and colleagues who play different, but still influential, roles in your life.

Perhaps, in the course of your discussion, you can use your list to tell your fiancé about the important and influential people in your life.

As you listen to your loved one talk about the important people in his/her life, ask that he/she use a photo album to show you his/her pictures. Try to file these names and faces in your memory bank. You can be certain that you will soon meet these people and that they, too, will become a part of your life.

What is your greatest fear?

Usually, when I pose this question to couples, I get one of two standard answers: "I am afraid of losing the one I love," or "I hate snakes."

But everyone fears something. Whether it's death or sickness or taxes, everyone has something that disturbs him/her. The problem with fears, however, is that they can cripple us if we don't master them. We need to talk about our greatest fears if we are to master them.

Couples who discuss their fears together will be prepared to face these fears when they become reality—which many inevitably do. Strength in marriage does not come from having an easy life but by working through the challenges, fears, and valleys of everyday living.

What keeps you awake at night?

Many people have problems sleeping when they are concerned about work, finances, or a new venture. Sudden changes in family or friendships can also keep us awake. Other people simply worry themselves sick by imagining possible outcomes to a problem—none of which may actually transpire.

Then there are those people who sleep like hibernating bears through the thick and thin of life, seemingly oblivious to the fact that the sky is falling.

Find out where your fiancé falls on the sleep-deprivation scale. This way, you won't be surprised when, the night before a big project is due at work, your beloved rises at two o'clock in the morning and begins to pace the floor.

What makes you angry?

Most couples learn about anger early in a relationship. But some are destined to learn about anger the hard way.

I read about a couple in Florida (this was back in the 1970s) who had decided to lay new carpet in the living room of their home. The wife insisted on shag carpet (at that time it was the latest craze). The husband, however, insisted that a short-nap carpet would be much easier to clean and manage. Refusing to give in to the other, each insisted on having the carpet of his or her choice.

One weekend, while the husband was away on a business trip, the wife ordered her favorite carpeting from a same-day carpet service and watched contentedly as the men unrolled and installed a fashionable wall-to-wall shag.

When the husband returned home to this surprise, he was livid. The next day, after his wife went to work, he brought the lawn mower into the house, fired it up, and casually proceeded to mow the living room! In a few minutes he had reduced the luxurious shag into a short-nap carpet.

That evening, the wife sued for divorce.

Before entering into marriage, discuss anger. Find out how each of you deals with your anger, how you vent your frustrations. If you need to explore this area more fully, try asking some of these additional questions:

- When you get mad, do you usually want to talk, or sulk?
- How long does it take you to cool down after you become angry?
- Have you ever become violent when angry?
- How do you feel when I am angry with you?
- How can I help you when you are angry?
- How can I help you calm down when you are angry?

What makes you laugh?

Good marriages are built upon smiles and affirmations, on laughter and happiness. Knowing how to make your future spouse laugh is a key ingredient in a fun marriage. Perhaps you can get a laugh with an old joke, a favorite story, or a gag gift. Some men laugh at *The Three Stooges* and double over in hysterics at the sound of a whoopie cushion. Some women giggle at the sight of a funny face and roar when they are regaled with stories about friends and family.

From the outset of your relationship, try to keep each

other laughing and smiling. Carry this good humor into your marriage and treasure it. The joy will serve you well in the years to come.

What is your political persuasion?
Are you a Democrat or a Republican?

At a recent parenting seminar I happened to find a husband and wife who were at opposite ends of the political spectrum. In spite of their political differences, however, they seemed to have a workable marriage. When I asked them about this, the fellow said, "We've learned over the years to talk about everything *but* politics. It's the one subject we avoid."

Regardless of your own political views, you can still have a loving and amiable relationship with someone adhering to a different political position. The adage that opposites attract has proven true time and time again, even when the point of contention is politics. Plus, with liberal Republicans and conservative Democrats littering the current political scene, you may not be as diametrically opposed as you thought.

If you find that political talk is too heavy or, for whatever reason, too emotionally heated, you can always come back to it another time—say, after you have been married for a few years.

How have your values and ethics changed over the years?

Remember: change is inevitable. People grow. People move out of one mind-set into another. This is true of everyone.

Not long ago I watched a television interview with a prominent religious leader. The interviewer asked the question: "Have you ever changed your mind about anything?" I think the interviewer was surprised when this leader answered, "Oh, yes! I have changed my mind over the years about a great many things. I have had new insights. I have grown in my understanding of many issues and my love for others. I am not ashamed to say that I have wavered on a great many things in life. And I am not the same person who made so many of those brash religious statements in my youth."

There is no shame in changing one's mind. Instead, it proves that a person is analytical and can consider other views.

What issues that we disagree on are most important to you?

This is a broad question, but it can arouse a depth of feeling in many people. As two people get to know each other well, they are certain to find differences of opinion on a great many issues. Some of these opinions will prove to be more intense than others.

A growing and loving relationship is one in which each person learns to understand the position of the other. There may not always be acceptance and resolution when there are differences of opinion, but a solid marriage is built on mutual respect and trust, even when one person believes the other is wrong.

Why not discuss some of these issues now? Get them

on the table in a clear and open manner. Such honesty and feeling can only lead to a more satisfying marriage in the long run.

How do you feel about abortion, the death penalty, euthanasia, feminism, homosexuality, racism, violence, sexual harassment?

Naturally this list could go on and on. Today, it seems, every time we open up the newspaper, there is a new controversial issue spanning the headline. Emotions can run high when we talk about these heated topics.

I know many marriages in which husband and wife have differing opinions on these issues. In fact, my wife and I approach several of these topics from different perspectives and understandings. In a world as vast and as diverse as the one we now inhabit, how could any of us expect to be exempt from differences of opinion? We will not always agree.

Sometimes we have to learn how to get along by agreeing to disagree in a peaceful and respectful manner . . . even in marriage.

In the event, however, that you and your fiancé cannot seem to reach an accord on some of the more emotional issues, and you find that you have reached a stalemate in your discussion, try to write your positions in a clear and concise manner. Exchange these notes and move on to another issue. Try to agree that, while you differ in your outlook and opinion, you can still respect the other's right to disagree. Then let it rest.

Love and Commitment

Whenever we think about marriage, we inevitably think about love and commitment. In fact, for most people, the thought of marrying for any reason other than love borders on sacrilege. Love represents the highest of human achievements and goals. And marriage is, in spite of ourselves, a wonder and a mystery of the highest order.

Often, by talking about our love for another, we begin to realize the true depth of our feelings and our commitment. May this be true for you and your fiancé as you discuss these questions.

What is your idea of a good marriage?

Good marriages come in all shapes and contours and varieties. Having an ideal, or model, in mind is often helpful to a couple as they begin to discuss the prospect of marriage.

William Penn said it well: "Never marry but for love; but see that thou lovest what is lovely."

As you think about this question together, you might use a pen and paper to write down some of your common ideals about the life you will share together.

What do you hope to receive from marriage?

This a good follow-up question to the first one. Our ideals of marriage are important. Some people hope for compan-

ionship. Others, sexual highlights. Some hope for the
pitter-patter of little feet. Others for financial security in
old age. One couple I married had this observation about
the question: "We have often thought of our marriage as
a foundation. From here we will build upward together—
enjoying each other's company, saving and planning
together, raising a family, growing old together. That's what
we want. We've talked about it a lot. And we know that
love is the mortar that holds it together."

Before you get married, it is good to know the expectations
of the other. In this way, you can be certain of trying to meet
those needs and desires that are important to your spouse.

What place will honesty have in our relationship?

Many times I find that people can be honest with others
but have problems telling the truth to the one they love.
There are many reasons for this. Often, when we do not
want to hurt another person's feelings, we will withhold
our own, or say something diplomatic, just to keep the
peace. Or when we are hurt, instead of lashing out in anger
at the one who has hurt us emotionally, we will yell at
someone else over an unrelated issue. When we are in love,
we sometimes want to spare the feelings of the beloved.

But the ability to share feelings honestly in a marriage
is crucial to a relationship's success.

One way to ensure that emotions are shared honestly and
lovingly is to formulate a set of questions that can help the
other person state what he/she is feeling. For example, you
might notice that your fiancé looks hurt by something you

have said or done. You could note the obvious: "You look hurt." Then ask if he/she would like to tell you what he/she is feeling. Give reassurance by stating "I'm listening."

If you are seeking to deepen the level of honesty in your relationship, you might begin by discussing a few of these questions:

- What do I do that hurts you?
- What do I do, or say, that makes you feel loved when you have been wronged?
- When do you feel unappreciated?
- When do you feel lonely?
- What habits or mannerisms do I have that bother you?
- How can I encourage you?
- What about me makes you uncomfortable?
- What do I do that makes you feel good about yourself?
- What do I do that brings you down?
- Do I need to offer an apology for anything I have done or said to you?

How can I know you will make me happy for the rest of my life?

F. M. Knowles once wrote: "Marriage is a lottery. But you can't tear up the ticket if you lose." And Montaigne is credited with the proverb: "Marriage is like a cage; the birds outside are desperate to get in, and those inside equally desperate to get out."

Throughout the centuries, marriage has been seen as everything from a necessary evil to a divine union. Most couples, no doubt, feel yoked somewhere between the two extremes. And as such, marriage has often been the butt of jokes.

But I wonder how many marriages would fare better today—especially in this age when one out of two marriages in America ends in divorce—if each one in the relationship paused to consider this question: How do I really know that this person will seek my happiness above his/her own?

This is the quality of true love. True love seeks the happiness of the other. Self-love seeks the happiness of the self. Many marriages revolve around the latter type of love. And then, as soon as one or the other member of the couple experiences an unhappy moment (which is inevitable), there is a parting of the ways.

But if you are looking for the kind of love that lasts, stand fast on this question. Make him/her think about his/her certainty. How does he/she know *he/she* will make *you* happy for the rest of *your* life?

Are we truly committed to each other for better or for worse?

Most traditional wedding vows ask couples to acknowledge that marriage is not easy. When a couple takes each other "for better or for worse," "for richer or for poorer," "in sickness and in health," and "until parted by death," they are recognizing life's imperfections, and the strengths and weaknesses in each other.

The question is not: "Do you love each other?" but "*Will you* love each other?" Marriage vows point to deeper commitments and ask couples to stay together no matter how wonderful or terrible life becomes. Most marriages, of course, contain a mixture—and couples hope that life will be filled with more pleasure than pain. In marriage, you will be helping each other create a shared life.

Make sure you discuss the depth of your commitment to each other. Couples who discover unwavering support, unfailing love, and unshakable devotion are far more likely to build a life filled with good things. Remember, marriage is a partnership. You are working together toward common goals, and the deeper your commitment to each other, the better, richer, and healthier your life will be.

How do you like to show affection?

How can any marriage survive without depth of feeling? Affection must be demonstrated in tangible ways. I like to remind couples that in marriage love is a verb and not a noun. Love must be lived out—it must be shown.

However, no two people demonstrate affection in precisely the same fashion. Some men, for example, are not high on the verbal scale. Others express their love with Shakespearean eloquence or through flowery letters. Still other men show affection through hugging, playful nudging, or by kissing. Some men bring flowers and candy on occasion.

Likewise, women are equally as diverse. Many women do not enjoy public displays of affection or spontaneous demonstrations of love. Others prefer to write letters or cards instead of talking. Some buy gifts or arrange a romantic evening at home.

If you have been in relationship with your loved one for some time, you probably have a good idea of how he/she demonstrates affection. But marriage can bring a different dimension to a relationship. Talk about your signs of affection now, so you will know what to expect later.

What is your concept of fidelity?

Some years ago I happened to see a talk show that featured a variety of married couples who were discussing their concepts of fidelity. One couple had arranged for another woman to be part of their marriage—a sort of concubine relationship in which the husband had his pick of two women. Another couple spoke of having an "open" marriage, a relationship in which both were free to explore their sexuality with others at any time. Still other couples offered a variety of interpretations of marriage and fidelity that bordered on the bizarre and, in many instances, the dangerous.

This is a good question to ask because the definitions of marriage and fidelity, for many people, have blurred. Fidelity is sometimes interpreted in ways that stretch the definition and significance of commitment and love. Be clear before you enter into marriage of your fiancé's concept of fidelity and be honest and firm about your own expectations.

What do you consider cheating?

Not long ago I overheard a conversation in the gym. Two men were talking about their wives. From the inferences I heard in the snatches of conversation, I could tell that one of the men was having an affair. "That's all right for now," the other fellow said. "Just don't get caught."

The line between fidelity and cheating has grayed in many people's minds. Like a teenager copying from another student's test, some feel that having an affair is acceptable, as long as one doesn't get caught. Others feel that it is all right to hug, kiss, or sexually arouse another person, so long as actual intercourse is not involved. Phone sex lines and pornography further gray the concept of "cheating"— and so all these issues should be discussed before marriage.

What would we do if one of us had an affair?

I once raised a similar question with an engaged couple in a counseling session: "How would you handle the reality of an affair, if one of you found that the other was cheating?" I was not prepared, however, for the verbal whipping I received from the woman for even entertaining such a possibility. "I won't discuss the possibility of an affair," she scolded. "We love each other too much. It's simply out of the question!"

I assured her that I was not suggesting that her fiancé *would* have an affair but was asking how she would deal with the situation *if* he did. Finally she conceded and shot back her answer, "I'd kill him! No questions asked!"

In the wake of an affair you may not resort to murder, but it is a good idea to know how you and your future spouse might handle such a situation. Personally, I know many couples who have survived affairs and now seem to have much happier marriages because of the communication and relational techniques they learned through counseling. Other couples, on the other hand, have self-destructed at the first hint of infidelity—no counseling, no dialogue, no second chances.

Discuss these feelings together. Talking about the possibility of infidelity does not heighten the chances that it will occur but rather diminishes the odds, since good communication has been established early. Knowing the depth of another person's love sets us free to return that love to the right person—our spouse.

Do you believe in professional counseling and would you be willing to go if necessary?

This is an important question in any marriage—and not just in cases of infidelity. There are periods (perhaps in all marriages) when the stresses and strains of life tear at the fabric of love and commitment. Doubt—or boredom, or uncertainty—can sometimes settle in. Just as individuals go through phases and stages of life, so do marriages.

Counseling can benefit marriages in a number of ways. A good therapist can teach techniques that can facilitate effective communication. A therapist can also give good advice when an intermediary is needed. Or, if there are problems with addictive behavior or abuse, a therapist can guide a couple to support groups and other agencies.

My experience as a pastor, however, has impressed upon me that, for many couples who find themselves in troubled marriages, one person refuses to seek outside help. This leaves the other person quite alone in his/her misery.

Try to agree, before marriage, that counseling will always be considered an option in your relationship, no matter what the problem, and that you will not give up on your marriage until you have exhausted all the avenues for saving it.

How do you feel about divorce?

As I have counseled couples over the years, I have noted that nearly 50 percent of the individuals have come from homes with divorced parents. And, in most of these instances, these individuals are always open with their feelings on the subject. In fact, there have been several times when one or both of the individuals have cried openly when talking about their parents' divorce.

Over the years I have noted that divorce knows no boundaries. Rich people get divorced, as well as poor. Deeply religious individuals seem to get divorced as often as marginally religious people or atheists. Older adults get divorced about as often as younger couples.

By now, there is probably no family in America who has not been touched in some way by the reality of divorce—a family member, a friend, a co-worker, a parent, a child, a brother or sister, a grandparent. It is a reality that has, in many ways, defined family and community for the past few decades.

Couples who are considering marriage need to talk about their own feelings on divorce—not as a possibility, or as an option, but to establish understanding and confidence in each other. Chances are, you will find yourself coming back to the hope and promise that you can live with each other until you are parted by death.

Are you able to agree to disagree?

There will be many times in marriage when you and your spouse will be unable to agree. But this does not mean it is the end of your relationship. Being the one who is right is not the most important aspect of marriage. Sometimes it is necessary to concede a point in a disagreement for the sake of peace. Forgiveness and concession go a long way toward establishing love and care for each other.

If you or your fiancé has a problem with disagreements or perhaps feels that you must always "win" an argument, spend some time talking about this question. Learning to agree to disagree is a giant step if you are seeking harmony in your future relationship.

Do you feel that you can tell me anything?
Are you able to express your feelings?

Difficulties develop in marriage when feelings are suppressed and communication regresses. A marriage will not thrive if a husband and wife are unable to express their deeper concerns. Superficial conversations and intermittent talks will make a marriage difficult to sustain.

Before you enter into marriage, make every effort to explore this aspect of an open and honest relationship. This will be at the heart of your love and commitment to each other.

Is there anything else that I should know about you?
Secrets are not good for a marriage. This is not to say that we don't have private conversations, thoughts, and experiences—but no one should enter into marriage with large skeletons hidden in the closet.

For example, you might ask:

- Have you ever had a drug or alcohol addiction?
- Have you had sexual encounters or sexual addictions I should know about?
- Do you have debt I don't know about?
- Have you ever been convicted of a felony?
- Do you have children or other family I don't know about?
- Are there painful experiences in your past that you feel you can't talk about?
- Do you feel that you can be vulnerable with me? Why or why not?
- How open do you feel we should be with our mistakes and weaknesses?

Do you trust me?
Do you believe I trust you?

A wonderful development I have seen in many marital relationships is the understanding that a marriage can be a union of best friends. And this is what marriage *should* be. This type of relationship is based upon trust and is the key element in drawing two people closer together as the years go by.

The first warning sign of a troubled marriage is when trust begins to erode. Once trust is destroyed, it is difficult to rebuild.

Infidelity is not the only cause of this erosion. Jealousy and overprotection are other trust-killers, as well as non-communicative partners, abusive words or actions, and addictions of various kinds.

From the beginning of your relationship, seek to establish open and visible ways of demonstrating your trust in each other. Seek to verbalize your trust as much as possible, give each other room to grow in other areas of life and provide opportunities for your spouse to be with his/her friends. Within the boundaries and goals you have established for your marriage, try to give yourselves permission to take some risks, such as with a business venture or by studying under a tutor. These types of opportunities will go a long way toward establishing trust in every facet of your marriage.

Sexuality

When counseling couples before marriage, the topic of sexuality always raises some concern. Because sexuality and sexual expression are typically seen as private matters, most people feel uncomfortable discussing this aspect of their relationship. I can understand their hesitancy.

Sexuality plays such a central role in marriage—particularly during the early years—that people naturally have doubts and insecurities about whether married sex will prove to be a natural high or an emotional letdown. These fears hold true for everyone, regardless of whether a couple has been sexually active before marriage or has decided to wait until after the wedding. Even couples who have had many sexual experiences before marriage harbor doubts about whether marriage will dull the spontaneity and edge of the sexual experience.

Couples hoping to make their sex life exciting and lasting will certainly want to discuss their feelings and desires with each other. I'm convinced that a great sex life cannot be experienced unless there is communication in and out of the bedroom. Couples who are able to tell their partners what they want are far more likely to receive the kind of love and sexual satisfaction they are seeking.

What kind of music, images, or scents get you in the mood?

If there is one distinct difference between the sexes when in the bedroom, it would involve the senses: men are generally stimulated by sight; women are generally stimulated by sound and smell.

In case you haven't figured out what sights, sounds, and smells are a turn-on for your fiancé, you might spend some time together at a cosmetics counter, sampling various colognes, or at a music store to find some mood enhancers. Or simply sit down and talk about it.

Also, try to remember what you learn from this question. A wise husband or wife, based upon this conversation, might figure out the perfect anniversary gift.

How frequently do you expect to make love?

A few years ago I conducted a marriage workshop for couples who were wanting to know how to make a good marriage even better. One of the areas we discussed had to do with sexuality and sexual expectations. I was surprised to discover that, for most of the couples in the workshop, sexuality was not a major issue. Most felt that their lovemaking was actually more satisfying and enjoyable after several years of marriage. Some made love more often after fifteen years of marriage than they had earlier in their relationship. There were several reasons for this.

A primary factor was the lower level of stress many felt after having been married for several years. For some older couples, this reduction in stress was because they no longer had to worry about conceiving a child; they were more relaxed and carefree. Others made mention of a more secure financial base—they could go to bed at night without worrying about work and were free to enjoy each other's company for perhaps the first time since their early years of marriage. Others mentioned better communication as a key factor in the frequency of their lovemaking.

The good news is: Sex can get better as the years go by. Love deepens, and couples are able to know, after years of experience, how to please their husbands or wives.

Early in marriage, however, is when many couples experience sexual doubts and insecurities. These doubts may arise more quickly once pregnancy or children enter the picture. A long day's work, looking after the children, keeping up with the new demands of home and family—all these factors can contribute to sexual inactivity in the initial years of marriage. Younger couples are often too tired to think about each other.

But this phase will pass. Great marriages and great sex lives emerge from these struggles, and the frequency of sexual activity often increases once these barriers are removed. Couples who make time for each other and talk about their sexual desires will find the perfect schedule for lovemaking.

Do you like to be spontaneous?

Movies and soap operas often portray sexual spontaneity through rose-colored lenses: a three-minute escapade in a moving elevator, a secluded moment on a crowded beach, a quickie in the backseat of a moving cab. While such scenes make for great movie fodder, in real life these types of liaisons would be difficult to arrange, even for a married couple.

However, great sex can be spontaneous, and it doesn't have to take place in the bedroom. If you want to talk about spontaneity in your sex life, why not talk about your fantasies in regard to where and when you would make love. Placing yourselves in these romantic locations later would go a long way toward making spontaneity possible.

Do you like to experiment?

Boredom and routine will kill a couple's sex life faster than anything. Chances are, you and your fiancé will not have to worry about boredom and routine for some time. But in the future, you may have to look to new approaches to keep your lovemaking fresh and powerful.

Before you get married, talk about some of the ways you hope to keep your sex life alive and meaningful. How might you experiment in your first year of marriage? Are there ways each of you could communicate and remember what you have learned about each other? These early experiences may help you to enjoy your sex life later on.

For example, you might recall that your spouse's sexuality was particularly heightened during your time at the beach, or that certain words or situations were especially powerful for you. Later in your marriage, you may find that attempting to re-create these moods, situations, or fantasies will help keep your sex life thriving.

How romantic are you?
How important is romance to you?
What is romantic to you?

Most wives claim that their husbands are as unromantic as clams. This could be the case, but I rarely see many wives arranging romantic adventures, either. Perhaps this is because we all get too busy.

But being romantic can mean just creating a space to say "I love you." Romance can happen in the home or in a special place. A romantic adventure can begin with a phone call of appreciation, a surprise candlelight dinner, a bouquet of roses or a new necktie, a note left under a pillow. Being romantic has to do with giving attention to the one you love. Words, aura, ambiance—all these can add to a mood or feeling.

Determine how much romance means to each of you. If it's important to one and not the other, it would help immensely to get expectations for romance levels out in the open. Also, find out what is romantic to your partner. A single long-stemmed rose is achingly romantic to some and hopelessly trite to others. Some men find background music and a bottle of wine romantic while others do not.

How do you feel about public displays of affection?

As a teenager I was painfully shy around girls—especially those I liked. I could never bring myself to hold hands with a girl in public and would show visible discomfort if a girl tried to kiss me. I am not this way today at all, thanks to my wife.

Often people who are dating have differences of opinion about public displays of affection. If you and your fiancé/fiancée seem to feel some discomfort in this area, talking about it might help you to gain a greater understanding of his/her personality.

Do you have any insecurities you would like to share with me?

Even in marriage, there are still personal secrets and fears. Everyone harbors feelings and insecurities that he/she finds difficult to talk about—even with a spouse. These insecurities are not necessarily sexual in nature, but they can often touch a relationship in such a way that sexuality is affected.

I once counseled a young married woman who was having difficulties relating to her husband. As we talked more about her relationship and her history, she finally was able to speak of the fear that was destroying her marriage. She had grown up in a bad home, with an abusive father, and now she was married to a warm and wonderful man who cared for her. Deep down, she felt she was undeserving of his love, that he was far better than she. She could not accept the fact that he really loved her and wanted her. She feared that he would find out how pathetic and unworthy she really was.

Issues of self-esteem, family abuse, and self-doubts often

surface in marriage. These insecurities can eat away at a marriage. But couples who take the time to discuss these fears will have a more fulfilling marriage and sex life, and will be able to support each other when these fears surface.

Do you feel sexually satisfied with me?
What do you hope I can contribute to make our sex satisfying?

Each person brings to marriage certain expectations about sex and sexual roles. For example, some women expect their husbands to always make "the first move." Some men hope that their wives will be willing whenever they are "in the mood." Many of these expectations have to do with stereotypes or misconceptions we have received about sex from our parents, from friends, from older siblings, and even from movies and television.

These misconceptions are often brought into a marriage. But they do not have to drive or control a couple's sexual experiences. Everyone can change and grow.

Talk about the roles each of you hopes to assume in your sexual relationship. Ask questions like:

- How should I let you know if I want sex?
- Who should make the first move?
- Do you like to talk during sex?
- Is it all right to do the unexpected?
- How can we let each other know when we are not in the mood?

What are your sexual fantasies and desires?

I am confident that, despite the saturation of sexual images and opportunities in our society, most couples have difficulty talking about sexual issues. If this is the case in your relationship, I suggest you and your fiancé use one or both of the following ideas to get your discussion going:

Write about a Sexual Encounter in the Third Person

Try writing a sexual scene in which you can picture yourself as a character. But, instead of using "I" and "you," use the words "he" and "she." For example, each of you might write about your sexual fantasy in the following manner: "When he came to bed, she was waiting for him. He pulled back the silk sheets and found that she was wearing the lace teddy he had purchased on their honeymoon. He reached down to caress her breasts and then began to passionately kiss the sides of her neck. She responded by pulling him close and . . ."

Well, you get the picture. Just have fun with your story, make it your own fantasy, and be sure to make your tale as explicit as it needs to be. Once you've written your story, you could attach it to a love letter, stuff it in a card, or simply talk about it. Or, if you want to be daring, try writing a story together about your honeymoon night.

Complete the Sentences

If answering a question about sex is difficult for either of you, and neither of you feels comfortable about writing a sexual fantasy, try this option. Take turns completing the following sentences (or make up others of your own!). These should get you started:

I like it when you wear _____

I like it when you kiss me on the _____

I like it when you whisper _____

I like it when you touch my _____

I like it when you do _____

I want you to wear _____

I want you to kiss me on the _____

I want you to say _____

I want you to touch me on the _____

I want you to tell me to _____

Children/Family

Most married couples, at some point, will want to have children. Marriage is certainly not defined by children, but children will forever change the complexity of any marriage.

I have been a parent for nearly two decades, and I can say without fear of contradiction that being a parent is absolutely the most thrilling, frustrating, joyous, perplexing, wondrous, and deflating experience of life. My marriage took on a new life and focus once my wife and I had a child. In a sense, we are still reeling from the realization that we are parents, uncertain of what to do in many situations, aware that we do not have all the answers to life's complexities.

Having a family changes the dynamics of a marriage in profound ways. Instead of a single relationship, a family produces several lines of love and bonding that need attention and care. Instead of a husband and wife focusing solely on each other, they must learn to focus on the needs of others. Parenting is, without a doubt, the one experience in life that teaches patience and self-sacrifice. Self-centeredness and attention to the petty details of life fly out the window once a child arrives.

The decision to start a family is a major step in any marriage. This is made all the more real by the fact that not all births are planned. Sexual expression in a relationship has its risks as well as its rewards.

I have never counseled a couple who had not talked about children before the wedding. Some couples decide that they want two children, others agree upon one, and still others want a large family. Some couples want no children. But the issue of family is always discussed.

As you talk about the questions in this section, I hope you will begin to consider some of the larger and more demanding issues of parenting and family life, especially as these issues will relate to your concept of marriage.

How many children would you like to have?

Few areas of marriage can cause greater consternation than a disagreement about the number of children one wishes to parent. If you want one child and he wants ten, someone is going to have to give at some point in the marriage. Experience tells me that the woman will usually get her way. After all, she is the one who must bear the load of carrying a child to term, surviving the pains of birth, and nursing the child. Reality dictates that, despite the father's most earnest promises and reassurances, the mother nearly always endures the majority of the late-night feedings, diaper changes, and colic cries alone.

Try to reach a decision about the number of children long before your wedding date. Although unexpected births do happen, it is an issue best resolved early, especially if either one of you has strong feelings about the size of an ideal family.

Would you ever consider adopting a child?

I have some good friends who decided early in their marriage to adopt a child from Mexico. For them, this decision was not due to an inability to conceive but because they wanted to make a difference to a child. I know that much thought and soul-searching went into their decision, and it was a complicated procedure once the paperwork began to roll, but they were blessed with a beautiful boy.

Listening to them talk about their experience with adoption helped me to see how difficult this decision was.

Couples who are considering adoption would gain much from talking to other couples who have adopted. In this way they can find out what adoption requires, understand more of the frustrations and heartaches involved in the process, and get a feel for the emotional ups and downs that the adoption process is certain to bring.

How do you feel children should be disciplined? Do you believe in spanking?

Bringing order and discipline to a family, teaching a child right from wrong, giving a child values and encouragement—these are the difficult tasks of being a parent. Every child needs boundaries from which he can learn proper behavior and freedom from which she can learn to express herself and grow. Without a proper balance of discipline and freedom, a child will not develop confidence and self-esteem.

If you and your fiancé require more information about child rearing and discipline, I would suggest reading any of the consumer parenting magazines which can be found in most bookstores. These magazines contain excellent articles dealing with a wide array of parenting concerns. No doubt you will also find many helpful books in the library or at a bookstore.

Keep in mind that, even though you may have definite ideas about discipline before you have a child, some of these notions may quickly evaporate once you find yourselves in a parenting situation. Children have a way of challenging even the most philosophical and well-thought-out approaches. I know parents who do not believe that spanking is an effective disciplinary measure; they rely upon other approaches. I know other parents who believe just the opposite.

Being a father myself, I often find that I need to talk about these issues with other parents. Experience has shown me that, when it comes to being a mother or father, on-the-job training is still the best teacher.

How are we going to handle birth control when we are married?

Today there are many birth control options for couples to choose from. However, I would suggest that you and your fiancé carefully consider the pros and cons of each method. Make a list of these options and weigh such factors as convenience, reliability, cost, comfort, enjoyment, and possible side effects. If necessary, discuss these options with a medical doctor.

For many people in our society, birth control is still a controversial and negative subject. For example, the Catholic church, in official teaching, condemns the use of artificial birth control devices or pills. The issue of birth control, for Catholic couples, may involve a discussion with a priest (see chapter 5, Questions to Ask Your Religious Leader). Other faiths may also have official teachings about birth control methods. This is not meant to be a condemnation of such religious ideas, but couples who are of these religious persuasions will certainly want to discuss the issue in an open manner.

For most couples, the main issue of birth control will revolve around the question: Who will be responsible for our birth control? Or, in other words, will you be looking at birth control from a woman's perspective (the pill, injection, diaphragm, tubal ligation, etc.) or from a man's (condom, vasectomy)?

I always like to remind couples, however, that no birth control method is 100 percent effective—not even vasectomies and tubal ligations. I know one couple who, after the birth of their twins, opted for a tubal ligation. Imagine their shock when, five years later, they learned that they were going to be parents again! The doctors told them it was a one-in-a-million chance that the ligation would not work . . . and they hit the lottery!

Family planning is wonderful, but be prepared for the unexpected.

What do you think is the woman's role and the man's role in a marriage?
Do you believe a woman should stay home and raise the children?
How do you feel about a man staying home to raise children?
Roles, expectations, and stereotypes need to be discussed early in a relationship, especially since these notions will play a vital part in any marriage. In addition to the issue of child rearing and nurturing, you and your loved one might also want to discuss the implications and practical

aspects of your various roles. You and your future spouse may have different ideas about career and family, and the way you are going to live these out.

Be aware that you will need to trust each other and rely upon each other's strengths once you become parents.

Will you change diapers?

Being a parent is not easy. Some tasks take us far outside of our comfort zones. But even the lowliest of tasks are often necessary.

If you and your fiancé cannot agree about some of the less desirable jobs, try to reach a compromise and divide up other parenting chores accordingly.

How active do you want to be in raising our children?

A friend of mine, a medical doctor, works incredibly long hours—sometimes as many as eighty hours a week. He and his wife made a decision early in their marriage that she would be the primary caregiver for their two children and he would devote most of his time to building his medical practice. This decision is not without ramifications, as they both realize.

Now they are facing a new challenge—that of trying to pare back the number of hours my friend spends in the medical office and hospital. Although his work is rewarding—both emotionally and financially—he is beginning to see the need to spend more time with his wife and children. He longs to become a more active parent, rather than just the breadwinner.

Every couple must make similar decisions all along the parenting road. If you and your fiancé intend to discuss these aspects of your future, these additional questions might help:

- How much time do we want to spend with our children each week?
- What priorities should we establish now, before we have children?
- What are we willing to give up in order to have more time with our children?

Questions for Interfaith Couples

In what faith will we raise our children?
This question might prove to be a central issue for your children at some future time, so it is wise to talk about it before marriage. When considering this question, you might also consult chapter 5, Questions to Ask Your Religious Leader.

Children begin to ask faith questions at an early age. However, they may not sense the nuances of religious belief that make one religion different from another.

Since most religious traditions have rites of passage for young adolescents (usually around age twelve or thirteen), you and your fiancé will want to begin talking about your religious traditions well before this time. If you want your child to adhere to a particular religious faith, you should begin training him/her in the early years. This will give your child a good foundation for understanding a particular religious tradition, with all the rites, symbols, and background needed to appreciate the depth of that particular faith.

How will we explain our religious differences to our children? And when?

If you and your future spouse have differing religious backgrounds, you will want to discuss the realities of religious education for your children. You may find that, personally, the two of you can work around your different traditions. But children often complicate the matter.

A good friend of mine likes to tell his own success story of growing up in a home with parents of different faiths. His father was a nonpracticing Jew, his mother a devout Catholic. After he was confirmed in the Catholic church, my friend went to a Baptist college, later became a professing Lutheran, and eventually married a nice Presbyterian girl. The two of them decided to compromise when they married and began attending a Methodist congregation. And that is how I met them.

When asked about his own faith, my friend would often say that he has a fruitcake religion—a little pinch of this and a little pinch of that. He sometimes calls himself a "Cathol-BapLuPresbyteriest." He credits his parents with giving him a firm foundation in faith, doctrine, and practice—but enough leeway and support to, when older, make an informed decision about his own beliefs.

If you and your spouse observe different faiths, come to an agreement before your marriage that you will respect each other's religious beliefs, especially in the presence of your children. This understanding will give you much peace and will teach your children the true meaning of love.

Questions for Those Who Have Children from Previous Marriages

How do your children feel about me?
What do your children say about me?
If you are marrying someone who already has children, your future spouse will naturally want his/her children to feel good about your relationship. Hopefully you will have many opportunities to talk about this aspect of your marriage and the needs of the children.

The role of being a stepparent is not an easy one. Make time to read as much as you can about the role of being a stepparent. In addition to the challenges and stresses, there are wonderful opportunities.

Also, talk about your stepparenting role with your fiancé. Ask about his/her expectations of you. Use some of these questions to dig deeper into this issue.

- How would you like me to help with the children?
- How do you see my role as a stepparent?

- What do you think your children want, or expect, from me?
- In what ways do you see me helping to discipline the children?
- How open can you be with me concerning your children's feelings and needs?

How well have my children received you?
What concerns do you have about my children?

Your fiancé/fiancée may have his/her own ideas about step-parenting, so if you are the one who has children, be certain your future spouse is informed about your wishes and expectations. Your loved one may have concerns about fulfilling a stepparenting role. Try to offer words of reassurance and be as forthright as possible about your own feelings and the needs of your children.

How can we help make our marriage a smooth transition for our children?

Over the years I have officiated at many wonderful weddings involving stepchildren. I have also seen some bad relationships. But I can always tell when the love that a couple has for each other has reached out to include children as well. The children have an aura of acceptance and security about them, and I attribute this to solid communication on the part of the parents.

Wherever possible, consult with other authorities, read

books, or talk with other couples who have children from previous marriages. Ask the tough questions and don't be afraid to discuss your doubts and fears.

Spiritual and Religious Practices

Even though I have officiated at many wedding ceremonies, I am often surprised by the depth of spirituality some services achieve. There are moments when this spiritual aspect surfaces in powerful fashion. Sometimes tears, laughter, and awe permeate the ceremony. It is as if we are somehow changed by the power of divine love.

Not only do couples want to experience this love, they also want to live within a spiritual reality that can guide them and make all of life more meaningful. Because everyone has a different way of expressing his/her spiritual beliefs and religious practices, it is vitally important that couples discuss this area of their relationship.

What is your concept of God?
We Americans have the most varied religious expression of any people on earth, and our concepts of God are quite important to us. Every poll taken in the past fifty years shows that the majority of Americans have a belief in a

higher power. We are a nation of churches, synagogues, mosques, and spiritual seekers.

In spite of this broad belief in the divine, however, most Americans consider their spiritual beliefs and practices a private matter. Outside of our worship places, people generally do not discuss their religious beliefs. This privatization can spill over into our most important relationships as well. Many couples do not talk about their concept of God until they go to meet with their spiritual leader to discuss the wedding ceremony.

Our concepts of God, however, are deep-seated and a part of who we are. Couples who have a deep faith in each other will want to discuss their personal notions of God. Doing so will open the door to many opportunities for continued growth together.

Why is your faith important to you?

I once asked a group of children on Sunday morning, "What is faith?" There were blank stares for a moment and then one little girl responded, "Faith is believing in something that you know ain't true."

Faith, however, is quite the opposite for most people. Faith has to do with those beliefs that we trust to be true. Judaism is based on the belief that the creator of the universe called the people of Israel out of slavery to be a chosen people, a light to the world. Islam believes in a beneficent creator who has spoken through his prophet, Mohammed. Christianity emerged from a belief that Jesus of Nazareth was God's messiah for the world. Even within these major religions there are variations and different beliefs.

Most people have a faith that sustains them in times of difficulty. Others have a faith that helps to mark the rites of passage—birth, adolescence, marriage, death. Still others have a spirituality that helps them to live in accordance with their traditional religious practices each day of life.

When you and your future spouse sit down to talk about your faith, you are certain to learn some fascinating things about each other. You will find out about family traditions, practices, and hopes, and the important rituals that will, no doubt, have a great impact on your life together.

If my faith differs from yours, will that be a problem? Why?

For some people, this may prove to be a difficult issue. Generally, the longer one has been a part of a particular religious tradition and the more consistent one is at practicing a particular faith, the more difficult it will be for that individual to move outside of that faith tradition. This does not mean, however, that two people from different religions cannot have a happy, successful, and fulfilling marriage. Perhaps just the opposite is true.

Couples who have interfaith marriages often have to work harder at communication and acceptance than those couples who come from similar faith backgrounds. Sometimes they have to overcome family or societal pressures to make their marriage successful. As a result, their love and trust deepens.

My advice to couples who come from different faith traditions is this: Keep the issue open for discussion, network the feelings of family and friends, and check with representatives of your respective religions. After much thought, you will know whether your relationship will bloom, in spite of your different faiths, or wither. Only the two of you can, ultimately, make such a decision about your future and the depth of your love.

In your religious tradition, what role will I be expected to fulfill?

A few years ago my wife and I attended a wedding ceremony and heard the bride repeat this vow: "I take you to be my husband and master of our home. I promise to love, honor, and obey you." Both of us were aghast, since the words "obey" and "master" had been expunged from most wedding ceremonies decades ago. My wife wanted to throw a rotten tomato at the groom, and I wanted to strangle the pastor. There is, however, a wide range of religious expectations that many people—particularly men—bring to marriage. Some religions or religious expressions do not accept the equality of men and women, nor do they use language that would appeal to most people in our society.

Some religious traditions (in Christianity, Judaism, and Islam) expect the man to be the "head of the home." This can be interpreted to mean anything from "I have a God-given right to make all decisions and knock you senseless if you don't agree" to "I must honor and love my wife."

Often, traditional roles in the home are carried over into the religious tradition and made into a kind of unwritten law. For example, some men will expect their wives to do the cooking, cleaning, and parenting—all because this is the "woman's role" in accordance with faith tradition. Other men might expect their wives to accompany them to any number of religious services, teach the children about the faith, or work as a volunteer to help recruit religious converts.

Over the years I've met fewer and fewer men with this mentality, but they are still out there. And, even though you or I might not choose to understand a faith tradition in this manner, such an understanding might be important to another person.

Before entering into marriage, make certain that you understand the religious expectations of your partner. It will save you a lifetime of heartache.

What religious practices are important to you?

As a child, I was taught to pray before meals. This simple ritual has carried over into my adult life, and I now teach it to my children.

Religious rituals and practices, whether simple or complex, can be important to daily life. You and your future spouse may not share the same religious practices, but it will be helpful to know what these rituals are and why they are significant.

Have you ever experienced a period of time when you lost your faith?

Some years ago I worked with a fellow who was a highly respected football coach. One summer he lost his coaching job after a particularly grueling season. Losing his job proved difficult for him to handle. He went into a depression, refused to eat or sleep, and gave up on his family, friends, and community. In short, he gave up on life itself. He also lost his faith in God.

It was several years later that this fellow regained his faith. But he first went through a difficult period when faith was nowhere to be found.

While my friend's plight might be extraordinary, I find that most people of faith go through alternating periods of deep belief and reserved doubt. A life of faith is more often like a roller-coaster ride than a one-way ticket to heaven. People who love each other find a way to lift each other up during these spiritual *down* times.

How have you experienced the presence of God in your life?

Life teaches us that our experiences are unique. Just as no two people would describe the same event in the same way, so our experiences of God will be different as well. This is true even for people of the same faith and religious traditions.

Some people find God in particular places—such as a church or synagogue or a quiet, majestic retreat. Others come to know the presence of God through particular moments—such as formal worship or a daily time of meditation. Still others experience God through other people.

Likewise, the way in which we describe our sense of God's presence varies. I have talked to people who define their experiences of God in stark, powerful terms. Others speak in a more subdued and introspective fashion, as if they are still waiting for further enlightenment. Some folks use traditional language associated with their religious heritage, while others seem open to new ways of speaking about the divine.

As you and your loved one explore your faith together, no doubt you will find that your experiences of God are quite different, but you may also share certain insights and religious desires. These insights can help you to find a religious tradition or faith that will work well in your marriage. Or you may discover that you prefer to focus upon your individual expressions and traditions.

What do you think happens to you when you die?

The subject of death and what happens to a person after death varies from faith to faith, from tradition to tradition. Some religions, such as certain traditions in Judaism, Islam, and most theologies in Christianity, believe in a physical death followed by the everlasting life of the soul. Other religions, such as Hinduism, profess an eternal cycle of reincarnations. Still other religions emphasize the eternal nature of the soul which passes from one plane of existence to the next. And there are other religions that emphasize the importance of right living, of pursuing justice and personal holiness, without regard for what happens after death.

To be sure, there is not enough space in this book to discuss all the various ideas and notions of death and the "afterlife." But you and your fiancé can certainly gain much by talking about your personal beliefs.

My own experience has shown me that concepts of an "afterlife" have little influence on the way people live from day to day. I know people who believe in a heaven with streets of gold and yet care little for others, and I know people who are atheists yet live by a code of ethics that would put many religious folks to shame.

What you and your spouse believe about a life after death, however, may make a marked difference in the way you deal with a death in the family, for example. Some people might see a funeral or wake as a time of mourning or loss. Others might view this time as a celebration of a life, an affirmation that the loved one has moved on to a better place. I am a Christian pastor and am always willing to share my own beliefs about life and death, but I appreciate and respect those who differ in their understanding of these faith issues.

By talking about your own beliefs, I know you will certainly gain a greater love for the one you are going to marry, even if you share different avenues of faith and understandings of God.

How big a role does religion play in your life?

As a pastor, I see firsthand how religion intersects with people's lives. For some people, religion is a peripheral concern. For others, religion is at the center of their lives. Or, to put it another way, their faith affects how they live from day to day: how they treat others, how they spend their time and money, and the manner in which they conduct business and enjoy life.

Having talked with other pastors, rabbis, and leaders of other faiths, I know that this same observation holds true for adherents of most religions. Not everyone is at the same place in their religious beliefs and commitments. This is not a judgment but an observation. Some take religious practice and belief with the utmost of concern, while others are content to find meaning in religion at certain times and stages of life.

In my own experience, however, I have also observed that religion does not always influence a person's code of conduct, ethics, and morals. I have known many "religious" people who are sour, angry, and abusive of others. Likewise, I have known atheists who seem to live by a higher code of conduct and love than many religious folks. Personally, I find more of God in the person of quiet faith and gentle service than the loud zealot or the boisterous cynic.

As you and your fiancé talk about the role of religion

in your lives—and how your faiths will be expressed within your marriage—make an effort to talk about the specific ways you each, and together, hope to practice your beliefs.

When and how do you like to pray?

Prayer can be a deeply private matter or a public act. Naturally, being a pastor, I engage in both. But prayer does not have to be a science or an art to be meaningful. I know many people who rise early in the morning for a time of prayer and meditation, some who retreat to a sacred location, and others who use ritual or repetition to pray a daily rosary.

But prayer does not have to be a scheduled event. One can pray anywhere, any time. Often the most meaningful prayers are those that well up out of some deep need, or out of a profound moment of joy or beauty.

As you and your fiancé talk about this subject, you might find it helpful to delve into some specific aspects of prayer. If this is important to you, try asking a few of these questions:

- When you pray, what do you usually experience or feel?
- When you pray, what do you normally express?
- Do you think we should pray together?
- If we have children, how will we teach them to pray?
- Will we have a family prayer before meals?

What gives you peace of mind?

It seems that everyone is searching for tranquillity these days. We live such hectic lives. Our calendars drive us from dawn until dusk. We are a seven-day-week people.

In the midst of that chaos, it is amazing that some folks have the ability to find a quiet moment to meditate, pray, or even think. Those of us who feel exhausted by the demands of the day might learn much from the ones who have a sense of peace, who don't seem to be losing their minds when we are losing ours.

It is good to know that marriage can provide opportunities for quiet moments, rest, and even privacy. Couples seeking this kind of spiritual satisfaction might also discuss some of these questions.

- How much private time will you require once we are married?
- How can I help you to find quiet time?
- What spiritual disciplines do you hope we can share together?
- Is there a special place that helps you in your spiritual life?
- Do you keep a journal?
- What books or literature have helped you spiritually?
- What has been the most profound spiritual experience in your life?

Past Relationships

Nearly 50 percent of all people who get married today have been wed previously. This is not meant to be a judgment, just a statement of fact. Many great marriages happen the second time around. Likewise, most people who marry have had many dating relationships over a period of time. They have made a decision to marry based upon past experiences and relationships that have helped them to determine the type of person whom they would like to love for a lifetime.

Marrying someone who has been married previously often involves a different set of questions. After all, there may be an ex-spouse to consider, children from a previous marriage, alimony payments, child care payments, and endless other possibilities. Marrying someone who has had many past relationships, or maybe even broken engagements, can also elicit a wealth of questions.

As I have talked to couples entering second marriages, I find that there are several good questions that are usually discussed. Sometimes these discussions are difficult. Other times they are delightful. But those couples who know each other well always desire to hash out the details of a previous marriage before entering into a new union. Likewise, couples who have had other meaningful dating relationships in the past often want to discuss certain aspects of this history.

The questions in this section will help you and your

loved one gain a greater understanding of these past relationships, whether you are entering into a second marriage
or have simply dated many people. Through these discussions, the two of you should gain a deeper understanding
of each other's tastes and lifestyle expectations.

How many sexual partners have you had?

I find that an increasing number of couples are asking this
question before getting married. For most, this is not necessarily a values or ethical question but a health concern.
Many young men and women today want to know if their
partner has lived a life of promiscuity. And if so, they want
to find out if they might be at risk.

This is not bad thinking. Not all states require blood
tests prior to marriage and, with the reality of sexually
transmitted diseases staring at us every day, a person is
certainly within the bounds of propriety and safety to ask
a question about past sexual relationships.

How have you been hurt by love?

I'll never forget my first adolescent crush. I was in the sev-
enth grade, had a bad case of acne, and the teacher had
assigned me to sit behind the prettiest girl in class. All day
long I would stare at the back of her golden mane of hair
and dream about being with her. Before the end of the
school year I had given her a ring—I didn't know why a
ring was so important, but it was something all lovers
gave—and I told her how much I liked her. The next day,

however, my ring came back with a note that read: "I'm sorry, but my parents won't let me keep this."

I don't know how I made it through the school day without crying, but I managed. For the next week I moped around like a wounded puppy and hardly spoke a word.

Love is a painful thing. We learn this early in life. And it doesn't get any better as we get older.

There have been many people who have been wounded by love. Hurt by parents. Rejected by boyfriends or girl-friends. Even dumped at the altar. It happens every day.

Your fiancé may have a deep-felt need to be assured of your unfaltering love.

Can you tell me why your previous marriage ended as it did?

If you are dating someone who is divorced, at some point you will want to know why the previous marriage ended. This is only natural. Not all people, however, feel comfortable talking about a previous marriage.

In spite of this, you owe it to yourself to gain an under-standing of your fiancé's feelings toward, and resolution of, the matter. Give reassurance that you are not judging, but listening. You simply want to know the reasons for the marital breakup.

But as you ask, do not assume that the breakup was ended with hard feelings. Expect the best! Not all mar-riages end in tragedy, animosity, or infidelity. The reasons for marital disintegration are as numerous as the couples themselves. And the best way to learn from and about previous marital failures is to talk about them.

How would you describe your current relationship with your ex-spouse?

Over the years I have witnessed a wide range of ex-spouse relationships. Some marriages end in such anger and animosity that the two parties seem unable to look at each other outside of a court of law, even when children are involved. Other marriages end amicably, with an understanding that is both affirming and loving toward all involved in the breakup.

In some instances there is no relationship with the ex-spouse—there is simply a parting of the ways, an understanding that two people are now free to pursue their separate lives. In other instances there is physical proximity to the ex-spouse which makes it inevitable that both parties will run into each other on a regular basis—in the grocery store, at the office, on the street. In other situations it is expedient, even necessary, that a person see or talk to his ex every day or so—to check on the children, to make arrangements for a child's doctor's appointment or baseball practice, or to plan a birthday party.

If you are planning to marry someone who has an active relationship with his ex-spouse, don't despair. Watch and listen. Try to understand the nuances of that relationship— what it is, and what it is not. If you sense that your future spouse has a strained or bitter relationship with his/her ex, it is best to ask how this animosity came about. The sooner you are able to work through your own feelings and needs with your fiancé, the better your marriage will be.

What is your relationship with your children from your previous marriage, and how will I be affected?

The decision to become a stepparent is an awesome step of faith and responsibility. I admire those who have the presence of mind and heart to make this added commitment at the outset of a marriage. The stepparent relationship is one fraught with many joys and sorrows, many delights and tears.

While I am certainly no expert on stepparenting, I have observed that many stepparents adapt quickly to the new role, and I often find that children from a previous marriage grow to love and adore a stepparent who shows tenderness, kindness, and understanding on a daily basis. We certainly can do without the classic understanding of the "evil stepmother." Children just want to be loved.

But as you enter into marriage, you will certainly want to talk about your new role as a stepparent. Often there is much apprehension and fear about filling this role, but people with big hearts are always suited to the task.

As you talk about this new role, you might consider these additional questions which will affect your stepparenting and your relationship with your spouse:

- How do your children feel about me?
- What role do you want me to play in disciplining your children?

- What should I know about your children?
- How often will your children be in our home?
- How often will you want to see your children alone?
- What can I do to be a good stepparent to your children?
- What do your children like to do?
- What do I need to do before our marriage to ease the transition for your children?
- What might your children expect of me?

Do you have any child-support or alimony payments?

For many second marriages, money seems to be a scarce commodity. It is an issue in our society as well. We read about "Deadbeat Dads," delinquent child-support payments, the huge alimony settlements of the rich and famous, lawsuits of every ilk and degree.

But the reality is much closer to home for most second marriages. In addition to the income required to make mortgage and car payments, insurance premiums and taxes, many second marriages are strained because of additional responsibilities.

Recently I read about one second-marriage family—a husband and wife who, after ten years of marriage, had three children of their own. However, the husband had two children from a previous marriage whom he was required to support. This couple had a strong marriage but felt weighted down by this additional financial burden.

Before entering into a second marriage where children

are involved, I often ask couples to sit down and make a financial assessment of their situation. It is good for a person to have an understanding of the financial aspect of any relationship before entering into it.

If you are considering a second marriage with children, you and your fiancé might use the following questions to gauge your financial situation:

- How much of your income will go toward child support?
- Will I need to earn a certain amount of income to finance the things we want?
- How do you want to organize our family budget?
- What additional financial responsibilities will I assume in our marriage?

Will you want to start a second family?

Many couples on their second marriage desire to start a second family, while others do not. The fact that you, or your spouse, or both, will become a stepparent should not deter you from asking about other children. You will certainly want to establish an understanding early in your relationship.

Naturally, starting a second family will have an impact on your marriage in a variety of ways. In addition to the new dimension children will bring to your marital relationship, you will also create a stepfamily (other brothers and sisters for your stepchildren). As with anything in family life, new possibilities bring joy and trepidation—all the unknown variables that one cannot adequately measure through simple conversation and planning.

But be bold and up-front about your wishes and hopes.

How did you handle confrontations in past relationships?

Everyone can learn from past mistakes . . . and successes! Allow your loved one an opportunity to talk about what he/she has learned about solving disagreements. As you listen, try to envision how you would have resolved a similar confrontation. Think about the ways in which your techniques might differ from other people's. This type of listening can help you grow.

If, for some reason, you perceive something in your partner's attitude or manner that disturbs you, bring this into the open, tell him/her why you are concerned, and see if you can resolve these differences. It could be that your fiancé needs to receive the benefit of your experience and problem-solving techniques.

Are you still in contact with a partner from a past relationship?

This question deserves explanation from a variety of angles.

First, in regard to an ex-spouse: If your fiancé/fiancée has children from a previous marriage, it is likely that, from time to time, you and he/she will need to be in touch with the ex to arrange transportation, weekends, etc. No one can live in a vacuum, and you should expect to talk with your fiancé's ex if children are involved.

If there are no children from a previous marriage, then contact with an ex-spouse may vary from person to person. Some divorces are amicable in nature, with both people harboring no ill feelings. There is still a friendship, even though the marriage is dissolved. Be aware that, if this is the case with your fiancé, you should not feel threatened by such a relationship. I know many people who have become friends with their wife's or husband's ex-spouse.

If neither of you has been married before, then this question can have a different complexity to it. Perhaps, during your courtship, you have noticed that your fiancé seems to have an infatuation with someone from a past relationship. Or maybe he/she seems to talk a great deal about someone he/she used to date. If this is the case, ask some other detailed questions that might help to clarify the situation: "Does this person still mean something to you in a romantic sense?" "Why do you talk about this person so much?" "Are you certain that you do not have strong feelings for this person?"

However, just because your fiancé/fiancée may keep in touch with people from past relationships doesn't mean he/she has no genuine feelings for you. It is only natural that, when we date someone for a length of time, we get to know that person well, maybe even develop a friendship.

This question might give you both a good opportunity to talk about the friendships you have developed with people of the opposite sex and why these friends are important to you.

Finances/Money

Finances play an important role in most marriages. This is a reality of living in a country where all things cost money. Without a steady source of income, stress begins to mount in a relationship. In many marriages, money is the number-one item that couples argue about.

Although most people would never admit to considering money a prime reason for marriage, standard of living is a major consideration for many people. I rarely see a wealthy individual marrying someone from a middle-class background. And it is equally as rare to see someone from a middle-class upbringing marrying someone who is poor. Perhaps this is not the way it should be, but this seems to be the reality in which we live.

The questions in this section will help you and your fiancé talk about some of the important issues affecting your financial future: what you hope to have, how you will manage your money, and your patterns of saving and spending. These are questions that will help you to budget wisely for the future and make your marriage work more smoothly.

How much do you expect to earn in the coming year?

You will want to begin any discussion of finances and marriage with a basic understanding of income. You will want to know how much your future spouse earns, and he/she will want to ask the same question. Once you have a good idea of how much you can expect to earn together, you will be able to prepare for everything from your wedding plans to the honeymoon and beyond.

Who will be the primary money manager?
Who will handle the household bills?

Before I was married, my mother gave me this advice: "There are three things you will argue about in marriage—time, sex, and money." How couples want to spend their time often causes friction. The frequency and desire for sex can also be a divisive issue. But money seems to cause the most problems.

Early in our marriage, my wife and I agreed on a simple plan—whoever could balance the checkbook was responsible for handling the household bills. However, after a few months it became obvious that neither of us could balance the checkbook. In a moment of reverse discrimination, the check writing and bill paying was placed upon my broad shoulders. For years I carried this awesome responsibility like a ball and chain. But then I discovered that I was able to use this job to my own benefit: through creative bookkeeping I was able to hide my own spending while amplifying the extent of my wife's spending habits. Now I have fun with my task: I am excited each time I sit down with the monthly receipts.

How you handle your money can make a difference in your marriage. Paying bills and managing your funds is probably one of the most important weekly affairs you will deal with. Take the time to find out who has the best financial head and go from there. You will have a much happier marriage if you do not fall into debt, bounce checks, or spend more than you are earning.

Who will be the "breadwinner"?

More and more I meet husbands who are staying home with the kids while their wives go to the office. I applaud these nontraditional choices and think couples should talk about these issues before marriage.

Think about your own relationship. Perhaps you are trying to determine who should be the primary income provider in your home. As you talk about this subject, consider some of these questions:

- Which of us earns more?
- Which of us has the potential to earn more?
- Which of us has the best benefits?
- Which of us has a job with the most long-term stability? Flexibility?
- Which of us dislikes his/her job the most?

How much do we have to earn to feel happy and comfortable?
Will we need one or two incomes in our marriage?

The decision about whether or not to find employment outside the home is a growing concern for many couples—

and not just women. I have always maintained that I would love to be a stay-at-home dad—if such a thing were financially feasible. I love spending time with my children and would welcome having that kind of relationship with them.

Early in our marriage my wife and I decided that we would alternate her employment with the needs of our children. Over the years my wife has worked at full-time jobs, part-time jobs, or has stayed at home—depending upon the needs of our children. What has worked well for us may not work for you. But you should have an understanding of how your family and marital needs will be balanced by your financial picture.

Only you and your future spouse will be able to determine what you want from your marriage—both financially and in terms of relationships. One way to assess these priorities is to rank them from most to least important, talk about them, and then determine what you will each sacrifice or do to achieve them.

Are you primarily a saver or a spender?

Good marriages come in many combinations. Sometimes both partners are spenders or savers. Sometimes a marriage is blessed with one of each. Either way, you will want to know the basic patterns of saving and spending characteristic of your future spouse.

It is also true that some people can spend a great deal and have nothing to show for it. Others are thrifty yet somehow manage to have some of the finest things in life. Once your relationship gets to a firm plateau and you are talking about marriage, you will certainly want to discuss in even greater detail your total assets and net worth.

Are you in debt?

It is not easy to talk about money before marriage, since it's such a personal issue, but asking about debt is no silly question. I know people who live in quarter-of-a-million-dollar houses, drive expensive cars, and soak up posh surroundings, only to wallow in insurmountable credit card debt. Some people are on the verge of bankruptcy but refuse to admit it. And, yes, there are even some out there who look for marriage as a quick fix for their financial problems.

I read a recent study on credit cards that indicated only 20 percent of Americans pay off their debts each month. Many Americans live beyond their means. Others shuffle debt from one plastic account to another, hoping that one day they will be able to pay off the mounting principal and interest.

If you plan to enter into a marriage with someone who is in debt, you might also want to consult an attorney and find out how, legally, this debt may affect you in the event of your spouse's death, disability, or a divorce.

What will be our total debt entering into marriage and how will this impact us?

Before you marry, be sure to total all of your debt. No secrets. What are your school loan debts, credit card debts, car payments, mortgage payments, and even those late fees? Will you have additional debt related to the wedding and honeymoon? Now consider your income. Is your total debt going to be a weight on your marriage, or will you be committed, together, to paying off these debts? Can you pay these debts?

These are not trivial questions. They will prove, in fact, to be vital to the health and longevity of your marriage. Financial debt and income/money stresses are the number one reason couples divorce.

If you need help with budgeting or finances, don't hesitate to talk to a financial planning or tax adviser. But begin with open and honest discussion.

Will we have joint or separate bank accounts?

Typically, when older people discuss marriage (especially if they have both been married previously), they agree to have separate bank accounts. This is a wise decision because it saves their grown children a lot of worry and makes it much easier to keep track of social security benefits and such.

Younger couples, however, usually start off by sharing a bank account. There are advantages and disadvantages to this. On the one hand, earning and saving money together leads to a spirit of mutual accountability. There's the sense that everything is being shared. On the other hand, having separate accounts can be a good thing if a couple cannot agree on spending and saving patterns. Having separate accounts lends a firmer line of accountability and sets a financial standard for the marriage that may be more easily manageable than the standard joint account.

Weigh the pros and cons and see how comfortable you feel about using either method.

Who will be in charge of budgeting?
Can we agree on a budget before we get married?

Setting a budget is, perhaps, one of the most difficult things to do in a marriage. At every turn there are challenges, needs, and unforeseen expenses. Often a firm budget is difficult to maintain when you are still getting to know each other and learning about the harsh realities of owning a home, buying food and clothing for a growing family, and keeping the cars in working order.

I advise couples to set a budget in their first year of marriage, but they should also be willing to revise it after the first three months and after the first year. Agreeing on a budget before marriage might be difficult for some couples, but even if you just set up some general parameters regarding how much you are going to spend in the major areas, this type of goal setting is better than nothing.

Try to be realistic about what you are going to earn and what you will need to spend and save. Unless you are on a supertight budget, try to allot some money for yourselves from time to time. A nice dinner, a concert, or even a movie can help break up the routine.

What do we anticipate will be our largest expenses in marriage and what is our plan to pay for them?

There is much to consider in this question. Budgeting will be crucial to your future. Be sure to consider the cost of health care insurance, your school debts, your mortgage (or rent), and car payments. Tally up your largest expenses (be *honest* and *accurate* in your figures). If there are other expenses related to prescriptions, treatments, or injuries, be sure to list these as well.

Your budgeting will be your plan to pay for these expenses—and the most successful marriages have a budget, share in it together, and stick to it. Your budget will be your plan not only for paying your expenses, but also for saving for your future, for your children, and for your retirement.

Be sure to ask: "Can we work up a budget together before we get married?"

What kind of health insurance do we need?
How much life insurance do you think we need?

The issue of health insurance and affordable health care will dominate our political discussions and worries for a long time. Not having a health insurance plan through your employer can cause tremendous worry. You and your loved one will certainly want to talk about your health needs and the type of insurance you need to meet them. In fact, there are more and more companies that are refusing to cover spouses and children, especially if they have preexisting health conditions.

Before you get married, review your health insurance carefully and talk about ways you can get the peace of mind you need.

In addition to health insurance, you will also want to discuss life insurance. No one, of course, plans on dying, but if you care for each other you will want to make provision for this type of care in the event of death. There are many different types of life insurance policies. All of these can be reviewed with an insurance representative.

Even if you don't have a large policy, plan to carry enough life insurance to cover the cost of a funeral. I recently asked a funeral director to tell me how much the average funeral cost. I was staggered by the $7,000 price he quoted! With these types of costs in mind, a couple should take special care to cover themselves in the event of death.

Care should also be taken to update life insurance needs every five years or so, especially if you have a growing family.

When should we begin planning for retirement?
How will we save for retirement?
What kind of lifestyle do you hope to enjoy in retirement?
Financial planners tell us that couples can never start planning for retirement too early. In fact, money placed in individual retirement accounts and company pension pro-

grams will earn far more for a young couple since the monies have more time to accrue interest.

If you and your fiancé are in your early twenties, or even your early thirties, retirement can seem aeons away. But most financial planners point out that couples who begin planning for retirement from the inception of their marriage will have a greater chance of reaching their retirement goals and dreams than those couples who wait until later.

Many younger couples have difficulties talking about retirement, or even thinking about it. But even a little bit of planning early in those first years of marriage can make a huge difference later on.

The beginning of marriage is actually the best time to talk about your hopes and dreams for every stage of marriage. If retirement seems too far away, why not ease into those golden years by talking about your goals for this stage of your life. By asking a few of these questions, you and your fiancé should be able to create a journey that will be both fulfilling and fun.

- What do you hope we can have when we are in our forties? Fifties? Sixties?
- What do you hope our marriage will be like after we have been married ten years? Twenty-five years? Forty years or more?
- What are your hopes and dreams for our children?

Household

Making a home together is what marriage is all about. But to do this well requires attention to many small details: everything from cleaning and cooking, to errand running and making sure the pets have fresh water. Couples who overlook the little things often find themselves in trouble with the larger issues of life.

The questions in this section will help you and your future spouse shape the decisions that will make your married life less troublesome. Here you can discuss all the mundane matters inherent in making your house a home.

How do you see us dividing the household chores?
Notice that this is a proactive question. Never ask your partner *if* he or she wants to do the chores. Play it smart and do not offer a choice.

Make it clear that you will be bearing your share of the load, but you expect your fiancé to carry out some of the daily chores as well. Couples who plan ahead and come to an agreement about household chores before marriage seem to have far fewer disagreements about the little things in life.

After all, once you begin to handle each other's dirty underwear, you realize that your love is truly sincere.

Do you like to cook?

I like this question, but it could be asked more forcefully: Will you do the cooking?

Just a year ago my wife took a full-time job outside the home, and I was forced to make a major shift in my household duties. In addition to taking the children to school each day and picking them up in the afternoon, I also began cooking the evening meals. At first it was rough going for all of us. Dinner consisted of Hamburger and Tuna Helper on a rotating basis garnished with a fine selection of canned vegetables and fruits. But then I discovered that I like to cook. My family struck gold because they loved my cooking.

If one of you likes to cook, this might be the perfect way of expressing your love. If neither of you enjoys the task, perhaps you could draw straws, take turns, or eat out more often.

Do you like to keep a clean house?
How often do you clean?

I have a couple of women friends who are much like the original odd couple. One is a neat freak; the other is unconcerned about dirty laundry, dust, or unsightly messes. They have roomed together for years and have somehow managed to stay the best of friends despite their differences in the cleanliness department.

As a married couple, you will be far more than roommates. But men and women often have varying opinions about what constitutes a clean house. Sometimes it is necessary for couples to work out these differences so that they can live comfortably together without constant bickering.

Who will handle household jobs and errands?
Who will take care of maintenance around the house?

One good way to divide up the household responsibilities is to make a list of the various chores and errands that will be needed to run your home on a weekly and monthly basis. You and your future spouse can then choose from or divide up these responsibilities as you think best.

If you have difficulty coming up with a list of your own, consider some of the weekly and monthly errands listed below. Each of you could sign your name next to the chores you would be willing to assume.

grocery shopping
auto maintenance/oil change
vacuuming
dusting
washing the dishes
washing windows
changing lightbulbs
collecting/taking out the garbage
recycling waste
cleaning the bathroom
yard work/leaf raking
mowing the lawn
preparing meals/setting the table

changing bed linens
laundry
ironing

What special touches will make our home feel warm to you?

The personal touches we add to our homes breed a feeling of love and serenity. Some people have a favorite rocker for reading, a beanbag chair for watching television, or a favorite photograph or painting they like to hang over the piano. Thinking about these personal touches before you get married will help you to plan your home together. Perhaps you can decorate some rooms as a team and others individually, with opportunities for each of you to express who you are.

Thinking about decor will also give you an opportunity to talk about furniture, the color of your walls, fixtures, the layout of each room, and the special touches you hope to add. Perhaps you can include a place for individual collections of art, antiques, or books.

A fantastic way to get ideas for your home is to subscribe to an interior decorating magazine or a specialty publication such as *Better Homes & Gardens*. If the two of you are into decorating, you are certain to find many usable ideas in books and magazines. Working together, you can transform your house or apartment with a special touch of class, warmth, or romance.

Miscellaneous
(and Personal Tastes)

Do you like to travel?

Not everyone enjoys riding in a car, streaking across the continent in a jet, or sailing the ocean on a yacht. Some folks are homebodies; they prefer to keep their feet on the ground and revel in being in familiar territory.

Take the time to share your travel stories and philosophies with each other. You may begin dreaming of some exotic places you could visit together or find yourselves planning your first vacation.

In the event that one or both of you hates to travel, you could begin thinking about shorter trips or other ways you can spend meaningful time together without traveling great distances.

Where would you like to honeymoon?

If you have not yet made your after-wedding plans, spend some time on this question. Remember: Big honeymoons cost big bucks. Unless you've been saving a long time for a two-week stay in Hawaii, you're going to kick off your marriage with some serious debt. That's not a good way to begin.

And, while the honeymoon is a wonderful, carefree time for newlyweds, it certainly isn't the peak of marital bliss. The best is yet to come.

Leo Tolstoy, in *War and Peace*, had Natasha say these words: "How stupid people are to say that the honeymoon is the best time. On the contrary, now is far better." Old Leo may have known a few things about life. Honeymoons are important (and should be planned accordingly), but what happens in the weeks following is far more crucial to a marriage.

If you want to get more specific about your honeymoon plans, ask some of these questions:

- How much do you want to spend?
- How long should our honeymoon be?
- What are some of your fantasies for our honeymoon?

What are some of your favorite books (or authors)? Don't be surprised, ladies, if your man wears a blank expression when you ask this question. Most men are not avid readers—women buy most books and magazines.

But if reading and literature hold an important place in your life, don't hesitate to ask the question. Sometimes women are surprised to find that their men know how to pronounce Dostoevsky and can discuss some superb novels in depth. A common love of books can be a lifelong hobby. I know several couples who spend time each week in bookstores or libraries.

Such places, incidentally, are naturally romantic.

Do you like pets?

Believe it or not, the issue of pets can be a touchy one in the home. I grew up with house pets (dogs); my wife did not. Now she wants a cat, but I'm not crazy about felines. Oh, well. We'll work something out.

Another aspect of pet ownership to consider: allergies. If your loved one has a tendency to blow his nose every time he visits your apartment, he might not be coming down with a cold. He might be having a reaction to your cat.

If you have a favorite pet but your future spouse is not crazy about having an animal around the house, this might be a sore point. In fact, if you are in love with your dog, you might have to choose between an animal and the man/woman of your dreams. It's been known to happen.

How do you keep fit?

One look at your future spouse and you should have a good idea about his/her exercise and eating habits. That roll in his belly might not be muscle.

If staying fit is important to you, then it will hopefully be important to your loved one as well. Some couples find that they are able to stay in better shape when they decide to exercise together. Taking walks, jogging, lifting weights, aerobics classes—all these are activities that couples can do together. Exercise can be fun, and it's even more enjoyable when couples make a commitment to stay fit together. You might find that some of your best moments in marriage are made possible by being in great shape: climbing to the top of a mountain together, hiking to a remote spot, swimming at a romantic resort.

And don't forget lovemaking. Those who are in great shape enjoy great sex!

What television shows do you enjoy watching?

In most marriages, the basic form of evening entertainment consists of watching television. You probably already know what shows your fiancé likes, but it doesn't hurt to ask. Your beloved may be missing his/her favorite one because he'd/she'd rather spend time with you.

However, if you never miss *Mad Men* and your fiancé enjoys watching only *Sunday Night Football*, you may need to sit down with the *TV Guide* every week to work out who gets to watch what when. Or an investment in a DVR may be in order to keep the peace.

What are your favorite colors?

Psychologists tell us that certain colors provoke feelings, desires, or latent urges. I don't know if I've experienced such a phenomenon in marriage, but it is definitely true that men and women have their favorite colors.

This question has deeper implications. The answer can affect everything from your house (inside and out!) to your car to your wardrobe. And don't be surprised if you can't agree on what color of the rainbow is best. Men and women do not always see eye to eye on color schemes and wallpaper patterns.

Knowing the favorite color of the one you love has some definite advantages. Buying clothing is much easier, and when you are looking for some impractical item for a birthday or anniversary present, you can always fall back on something in a favorite hue.

A respect for colors certainly helps contribute to a colorful marriage.

What are your hobbies?

Not everyone is a stamp collector. Some folks have unusual and fascinating hobbies. One fellow I know likes to grow herbs and make his own specialty vinegars. Another woman makes old-fashioned, decorative chalkboards. And one gentleman toastmaster I know is a collector of quips and quotes—he sends me a monthly supply of these verbal gleanings along with his own cartoon drawings.

Hobbies can be something a husband and wife can share or pursue separately. I've met plenty of couples who found each other at Star Trek conventions, writers' clubs, and sports outings. Common interests are still one of the binding forces of any meaningful relationship.

What is your morning routine?

If you don't already know your future spouse's morning routine, you should definitely find out. All of us have our own idiosyncrasies—from the way we rise from bed to the way we brush our teeth and eat our breakfast. Some people are morning glories—up with the sunshine with a smile on their faces. Other folks rise as if shaken from death and do not come alive until after the first cup of coffee or the completion of the morning paper.

Rituals are important to our lives. Without these morning rituals, in particular, we would be late for work or school; breaks from routine are especially disorienting at this groggy time of the day. My wife and I have developed such a highly refined ritual of rising, showering, and dressing that we barely acknowledge each other until after we have finished breakfast. And we like it that way!

Knowing what to expect from your spouse in the morning will help you both to get off to a good start. If either of you is not a morning person, you should make this clear up-front.

P.S. This tip might save your honeymoon.

Do you like to shop?

I tossed this question in the bag because many women enjoy shopping and love to watch a man's reaction when he is asked. I've met few men who like to shop with their sweethearts. Some submit to the torture out of obligation, though most view it with mortal dread.

As one female power shopper observed: *Men don't shop—they buy.*

If, by sheer dumb chance, you happen to have a man who prefers the mall to the recliner, or if both of you share an equal fascination or disdain for shopping, count your blessings. There is no doubt that you will have one of the most blissful marriages ever.

Do you snore?

Another *must* question—particularly if you are a light sleeper yourself and want to get any rest at all. Be warned, however. Snorers are usually quite sensitive to their plight and rarely admit that they sound like a locomotive.

The best way to find out if your loved one snores is to ask close friends and relatives who have known the poor sucker for ages. Chances are, if they have slept within proximity of your loved one, they will know the truth.

Snoring can be a problem, especially in marriage. I know a few couples who sleep in different bedrooms. Some wear earplugs. A few have resorted to surgery or found relief in inexpensive nose clips.

If you find out that your future spouse is a snorer, don't panic. Just give some calming reassurance and let him/her know that you will love him no less, even with his/her malady. Working together, you should be able to find a solution that can ensure a good night's sleep.

A Few Closing Comments

H.W. Longfellow once wrote:

> *"The men that women marry,*
> *And why they marry them, will always be*
> *A marvel and a mystery to the world."*

I hope that the questions in this section have helped you uncover some of the mysteries of love, have helped you to discover some of the lovely and generous qualities that are unique to the person you cherish. Some of the questions, no doubt, were more helpful than others, and perhaps the ones raised in this book have prompted you to ask other questions of your own.

If, however, after reading through the many questions in this section, you find that there are other topics you would like to discuss with your future spouse, why not glance through this additional list of questions. You might find just the right query for a special situation.

Additional Questions

- What foods do you like?
- What is your favorite restaurant?
- What is your favorite season of the year?
- What is your favorite musical group?
- Who is your favorite singer?
- What is your favorite movie?
- Do you play any musical instruments?
- What were you like in high school?
- What kind of a student were you?
- What subjects do you wish you had taken in school?
- What are your brothers and sisters like?
- What is your favorite thing to wear?
- What kind of bed is most comfortable to you?
- Are you a morning person or an evening person?

- What are your favorite card games?
- What is your favorite sport?
- What is your favorite beverage?
- Who is your favorite entertainer?
- What kind of car would you drive if you could afford anything?
- What are your favorite places to visit?
- Who are some of your best friends?
- Do you like to sing?
- Do you know any card tricks?
- How much and how often do you give to charity?
- How often do you serve as a volunteer for charity?
- Have you ever served in the armed forces?
- Are you a writer?
- Do you have any mechanical abilities?
- Are you on any social media sites?
- What else do you do on the Internet?
- Have you ever been involved in a car accident?
- Have you ever been mugged?
- Have you ever dieted?
- What's the best thing that has happened to you in the past year?
- What's the worst thing that has happened to you in the past year?
- What is your favorite memory?
- What magazines do you enjoy reading?
- How do you like your coffee?
- What's the most money you've ever made in a year?
- Are you good at balancing a checkbook?
- What is your favorite holiday?

- When do you like to take vacation?
- Do you prefer warm climates or cold?
- Who was your first girlfriend/boyfriend?
- What's the worst thing you've ever seen?
- Have you ever gone on a blind date?
- Have you ever had a life-threatening illness?
- Have you ever hit someone?
- What's the longest you've gone without sleeping?
- How would you describe our first date?
- What do you like best about me?
- If you could change one thing about me, what would it be?
- How would you describe me to someone else?
- How would you describe my personality?
- Why do you think we are a good match?
- Who has the best marriage you've ever seen?
- Do you have any tattoos?
- Have you ever committed a felony?
- Have you ever gotten a speeding ticket?
- Have you ever taken a night class?
- Have you ever moonlighted on a second job?
- What's the worst job you've ever had?
- What's the best job you've ever had?
- What style of furniture do you prefer?
- What color would you prefer our bedroom to be?
- What do I do, or say, that turns you on sexually?
- What do I do, or say, that is a turnoff?
- What is your favorite perfume?
- What's the craziest thing you've ever done?
- What's the longest you've gone without eating?

- How many books do you read in a year?
- Have you ever had to take care of an aging parent?
- Do you collect anything?
- Have you ever received an award?
- Do you have any trophies?
- How many weeks of vacation do you receive each year?
- How do you like to wear your hair?
- How do you like me to wear my hair?
- How much do you expect to spend on entertainment each month?
- Do you know anyone who is famous?
- What is your ring size?
- Do you like to camp?
- Do you like to have your picture taken?
- Do you enjoy meeting new people?
- What is the best present you've ever given?
- What is the best present you've ever received?
- Can you recite any poems from memory?
- Do you speak or read any other languages?
- Do you have any relatives living in other countries?
- What do you know about your ancestry?
- Do you have health insurance?
- Do you have life insurance?
- Do you like to fly?
- What is the longest you have lived in one place?
- What subjects do you like to avoid?
- Do you have any enemies?
- Have you ever done any acting?
- Have you ever been in jail?

- What do your parents think about me?
- What do your friends think about me?
- How would you describe our relationship to a good friend?
- Are you currently doing what you enjoy?
- Do you see a career change in your future?
- Do you have any sexual difficulties I should know about?
- What elements of the wedding are most important to you?
- Is diet and exercise a part of your lifestyle?
- How much time do you spend online? Watching television? On the phone?

CHAPTER TWO

QUESTIONS TO ASK
YOUR FRIENDS AND FAMILY

Marriage is a lottery,
but you can't tear up the ticket if you lose.
—F. M. KNOWLES

There's an old adage: Love is blind. And how accurate that maxim is! Sometimes our love for another person can blind us to that individual's flaws and destructive habits, or we can fail to recognize the highest qualities of that individual. We simply cannot see or know the fullness of the person we love because we're so close that we can't be objective.

That is why, before entering into marriage, it is good practice to have an open and honest discussion with your friends and family about your future spouse. Ultimately their opinions may not influence your own, but you can be aware that every relationship touches and changes the nature of other relationships. It is also true that friends and family (whose opinions you value) can sometimes provide insights you could never obtain on your own. They are able to see through different eyes and hearts—and may even have opinions more forgiving than your own.

Some years ago I conducted a class for parents of adolescents. Many of these parents were just beginning to agonize over the choices made by their teenagers. Some were concerned about drugs and alcohol, others about their teen's driving. But every parent was concerned about their son's or daughter's dating relationships.

As we explored this concern, I discovered that most of the parents were far more forgiving and rational toward their teenagers' dates than their teenagers seemed to be.

One mother expressed her concern this way. "My daughter has dated many fine young men, and a few losers. But for some reason, at least in my mind, she seems to focus on the wrong things. My daughter is overly concerned about good looks and nice cars. If a boy doesn't spend money on her, she dumps him. I've been very impressed with a few of the boys who have come to our home. They are polite, have values and wonderful personalities. But my daughter just wants a studmuffin with a new car."

"It's not only teenagers who act this way," one father interjected. "I think we have to take some responsibility for the atmosphere we've helped to create. After all, I drive a nice car. So my son will naturally want to drive a nice car. And everything in our society celebrates the body. Teens are naturally drawn to anything glamorous and beautiful. They want it, too."

"My sister is thirty-seven years old," one fellow added.

"And she can't make up her mind about men, either. I've been impressed with some of the men she has dated, but for some reason she always finds fault in them. No one is perfect. Sometimes I think it's easier for us to be objective about another person if we are a bit removed. When we're in the relationship, it's sometimes difficult to judge clearly."

Leading that parenting class taught me a great deal about the nature of love. The people who love you only want the best for you, which is why you should listen, even when they're saying things you don't want to hear. You don't have to agree; just be open-minded enough to absorb what is being said.

Consider the helpful feedback your own family has to offer you. Your family might perceive many wonderful traits in your fiancé that you have overlooked. Sometimes family members can be a positive source of affirmation and can help us to clarify a relationship.

Likewise, your family might be able to forecast problems long before you can. Family members have the luxury of being able to observe from a healthy distance. They might see subtle facets of your relationship that are like blind spots in your vision. Or they might see those destructive aspects of your loved one that may hint at future problems.

How often have you found yourself commenting to another family member, "I don't know what she sees in him?" We know that we see other people's marriages in a different light than the couples themselves. Why should we expect our own relationship to be any less transparent?

As you consider questions you should ask your family, don't forget to elicit additional help from your closest friends.

A good friend might have the advantage of knowing your loved one longer and better than any of your relatives.

For example, perhaps your fiancé was part of a circle of friends who shared grade-school and high-school years together. Or maybe you have friends who have worked with your loved one . . . or even dated him/her at one time. One of your old and respected friends might be able to tell you far more about your fiancé than any family member.

However, given the transient nature of American society, it is becoming increasingly difficult to know *anyone* for a long period of time. Many men and women do not have long-standing friends and childhood relationships to draw upon. The best they can do is network among the friends they have found after taking a new job or moving to a new community.

Many men and women feel disconnected from others. But this reality alone is good reason to seek out the opinions of friends—even if they are relatively new friends. In doing so, we discover that the world is much smaller than we think.

I have known women who have met men they thought were wonderful in coffee shops or at church functions, begun a serious relationship and eventually decided to marry, only to discover that the man they thought they knew so well was actually a reputable womanizer, a convicted felon, or a part-time drug dealer. Likewise, I've known men who have been equally surprised to discover that their sweethearts were fooling around on the side or had been involved in illegal activities. These things do happen, but they could be avoided if men and women would take the time to ask a few more questions.

Before entering into marriage, have a talk with your family and closest friends. You may be surprised at what you will discover about yourself, and your loved one. Most likely you will hear glowing reports and gushing feedback, positive affirmations of the love that you have found. These positive comments alone are worth the effort. Consider how wonderful you will feel when you find out that you have the blessing of those who love you best.

The questions you will find in this chapter are meant to give your family and friends an opportunity to express their feelings about the marriage relationship and, at the same time, elicit valuable insights that might benefit your marriage. You may shed a few tears together, share a few laughs, or enter into some deep discussions, but you will no doubt enjoy and appreciate what you will learn.

Do you think we make a good match? Why?

One of my favorite movies is *Fiddler on the Roof.* I especially enjoy the opening scenes when the daughters are singing to the village matchmaker. They want the old marriage broker to find the perfect man for each of them.

Of course, the movie and play reflect an age-old European tradition of pairing together boys and girls while in childhood or adolescence. Parents (usually the fathers) arranged the marriages for their children. Emotional and physical attraction were never considered. Love was not the aim of marriage. Rather, it was security and compatibility that were most highly valued.

But in the movie, one by one the girls forgo the ritual

of the matchmaker in order to find love. They do not want security alone. They long for emotional attachment and the joy of loving freely.

In spite of the fact that nowadays most people have never heard of a marriage broker, it is nevertheless true that most men and women long to find a good match in their marriage relationship. I have found that every person who is considering marriage loves to hear affirmations like: *You are the perfect couple! You were made for each other! What a perfect pair you make!*

No doubt your friends and family will have some positive insights about your relationship. Perhaps their comments will affirm what you have always known—that you have found the perfect person to complement your life.

What kinds of problems, if any, do you see us having if we get married?

During a men's retreat, one fellow shared this story about his wife:

"A few weeks before my wife [Cindy] and I were to be married, I went fishing with some old friends of mine. We were out in the boat, having a few beers, relaxing, when one of the guys asked me if I had told Cindy that I couldn't have children. My friends all knew that I had been infected with a serious fever as a child. I guess they wanted to see how I would respond.

"I told them that, no, actually I hadn't talked to Cindy about this, even though I had tried to broach the subject on several occasions. I just felt too embarrassed to talk about it.

"My friends got a few laughs out of this, but I think they were trying to help. And they did get me to thinking. Later that day Cindy and I talked about my inability to father children. She was supportive, and we discussed other options. But if my friends hadn't pressed the issue, I'm not sure what I would have done."

Through listening to your friends, you might receive some sage advice that you could carry into your married years. Perhaps you will find that there are aspects of your relationship that the two of you will need to work on or change. Likewise you might discover that there are pinch points in your relationship that you and your fiancé should discuss before getting married.

Few of us ever want to hear about potential problems. But confronting a *potential* problem *before* marriage is far better than having to work out an *actual* problem *in* marriage.

I know this is a good question (and a tough one to answer if it is asked of you) because I had it posed to me by a friend years ago. She had been divorced for five years, had two children, and was planning to marry a fellow who had been divorced for six years (without children). The only potential problem I saw in their relationship centered on his attitude toward her children. Whenever they were together, I noted that he seemed distant and uninterested in her two boys. I thought, perhaps, that he resented the fact that he was inheriting a family along with the marriage.

"It's funny you should say that," she noted. "Several other friends have mentioned the same thing."

The fact that she was able to recognize this concern,

and had been asking her friends about her fiancé, was a great boost to her relationship. Because of these honest responses, she could share this concern with her fiancé; they were able to reach a resolution and understanding of this matter before the wedding.

Consider your own relationship. Ask questions. Listen closely to your friends and family. Their responses could save you much heartache and anguish later on.

Have you ever witnessed my fiancé mistreating me in any way?

This is a good question to ask—especially if you are the type who seems to fall in love rather quickly.

One summer, while helping with an AA support group, I witnessed an ongoing series of jocular barbs and verbal jabs that a young man dished out to his girlfriend with increasing frequency. She seemed oblivious to this verbal abuse and even seemed to appreciate being the butt of his humor, but the onslaught was torture for everyone else to witness. At last, one of the women in the group took the young woman aside and gave her the score. "He's putting you down. He's making fun of you," she said. "Why don't you stand up to him? We're all here to support you."

The young woman's response was saddening. "I know he's trying to hurt me," she admitted. "But I know I can change him. If I don't act hurt, he will eventually get tired of teasing me."

"But how do you know?" the woman asked.

"Because my dad makes fun of my mom all the time."

This young lady seemed oblivious to the subtle digs and subversive taunts of the boyfriend. In fact, she considered them quite normal. And, in the end, she thought she could change her boyfriend by ignoring the problem.

Keep in mind—problems never go away by themselves. Difficult situations do not resolve themselves naturally.

Ask friends and family members if they have witnessed any types of mistreatment or abuse in your relationship. Hopefully you will discover that you have fallen in love with the one who truly cares for you.

What advice would you give me before marriage?

Several years ago I organized a marriage seminar for high school seniors. I invited grandparents, parents, and golden-anniversary couples to sit on a question-and-answer panel. It was a glorious event. I know I learned as much as those high school students.

The teenagers were invited to ask questions of the panel about a range of subjects. Some of these questions were light, while others were serious. Those sitting on the panel had a wonderful time reflecting on the various aspects of work, politics, and faith that had shaped their lives. The teenagers had as much fun as the adults. And they enjoyed the time so much, they asked the panel to come back the next week.

But by far the most enlightening question of the entire evening was: *What advice would you give me before marriage?* Here are a few of the more memorable responses:

- Never go to bed angry at each other.
- Save time to talk every day about the little hurts and pains; if you are faithful in the little things, your marriage will never be wounded.
- Find something you both like to do, and do it together.
- Don't let your man/woman get in the habit of watching television instead of paying attention to you.
- Make each other happy, and you'll never seek happiness with someone else.
- Never argue about money; decide on a budget before marriage.
- Learn to laugh at yourself and never take life too seriously.
- Spend as much time together as you possibly can.
- When you are young, you think life lasts forever. Actually, it is short; keep this in mind and you will never get too upset about the little things in marriage.
- The older you get, the slower you get; live it up while you can.
- Never lie to your husband or wife.
- When you are twenty, you live for sex; when you are thirty-five, you're too tired for sex; by the time you retire, you've forgotten how to do it.

If you want some sage advice, ask your grandparents or older friends to give you the benefit of their wisdom and experience. You might want to write down their responses. A journal makes a fine keepsake. And no doubt some of the tidbits you receive will give you a good chuckle or a heartwarming smile in the years to come.

How does my fiancé make me a better person?

Many of the highest ideals of marriage, and what you want from marriage, center on the desire that your spouse can complement you, can somehow inspire you to be a better person. This is the concept of the yin and yang, the idea that two people share strengths and thus minimize weaknesses.

Some husbands, for example, might help their wives learn new skills or might challenge their wives to travel overseas. Some wives might help their husbands to be more emotional or to give more of themselves in other relationships.

Sometimes love complements us in ways we could never envision. The fact that we choose to place the welfare of another above our own, to love for richer for poorer, for better for worse, in sickness and in health, moves us beyond self-centeredness. We can no longer be *just* individuals. We are changed by the very nature of love itself. The best relationships in life are marked by this: Psychologists and philosophers call it the concern for *other*. Growing together in marriage, changing together, is one of the marvels of existence. Love changes everything . . . and makes us better in spite of ourselves.

Is there anything you know about my fiancé you think I should know about?

Years ago, a question was asked of the congregation in most Christian wedding ceremonies: "If there is anyone here who can show just cause why these two should not be married, let him speak now or forever hold his peace." This line was removed from most ceremonies decades ago but is still used in many Hollywood movies because of its great comic possibilities. You have probably seen a number of movies in which someone in the congregation stands up at this point in the wedding ceremony and says something crazy. Witness *Four Weddings and a Funeral*, in which a deaf man stands up to protest the marriage because he knows the groom, his elder brother, is in love with someone else.

Historically, however, the reasons for this question date back to a time in which there were few public records, when a man might travel to a distant town to quickly wed a second wife or change his name or marry under false pretenses or while fleeing from justice. The question was meant to challenge such secrets, to ask for the assistance of the community in determining whether motives were pure, whether names and faces were accurate and legal.

Today one rarely hears the question at wedding ceremonies because we assume that our public records and massive communication networks make it nearly impossible for someone to marry under a false name, or to have two or three wives simultaneously.

However, this does not preclude people from keeping

secrets from each other. Many people marry each year and never learn about the skeletons in their partner's closet. Sometimes these secrets are known by other friends and family members. It never hurts to ask.

You might even learn a few positive well-kept secrets. Perhaps your fiancé is wealthy. Maybe he has a second home in the mountains or at the beach. You might learn that her company provides better health insurance than your company, or that she has a thick portfolio of stocks and bonds. Never assume that secrets are a bad thing. There are always good ones waiting to slip out.

How happy do you see us being ten years from now?

Planning for the future is such a major aspect of any marriage that it warrants the input of others. No one can live in the past. We must always live for the future. And for this reason it is wise to spend some time focusing on our hopes and dreams for tomorrow.

My experience has taught me that most couples spend far too much time discussing the problems and concerns of the near future (the wedding, the honeymoon, the next job) and far too little time discussing their hopes and dreams for the distant future (paying off a mortgage, rearing and educating children, planning for vacations and retirement). Couples who focus only on the near future, I find, have happiness for a time, but then it wanes in the passing years as these quick plans and goals are accomplished.

I always tell couples: If you are going to get married, strive for the biggest dreams you have and plan for them your entire lifetime. Don't focus on easily obtainable goals. Have a grand plan that will take you together into your golden years. That way, you're always reaching for the future, and the stars.

Family and friends should be able to offer you some valuable insights about your future. It doesn't take a psychic to figure out that our lives move in the direction of our dreams. Your closest friends may have valid reasons for insisting that you will not be happy with someone over the course of a lifetime. Perhaps there are areas of potential stress that you have never considered. Maybe there are disagreements that you have swept under the rug. Or you might simply be following your heart instead of your powers of reason.

What do you consider my fiancé's strong points?

Here's a great question to ask when you are out to dinner with your friends or family. Give everyone a napkin and a pen, and ask them to write down a top-ten list of qualities that they admire in your fiancé. No doubt this question will help you to understand exactly how everyone else feels about the one you love.

Don't despair. Even Jack the Ripper and Dillinger probably had a few strong points. If the answers seem slow in coming, or the ink doesn't flow too profusely, be patient. People often need time to search through their own experiences and understandings before they can articulate or write about them.

Once you have some positive responses, you will feel a

sense of pride and satisfaction for having chosen well. You'll have the strength and support of those you love and who love you.

And, if you save those napkins, you'll have a marvelous anniversary gift to share with your husband or wife some day.

What do you consider my fiancé's weaknesses?

Unlike the previous question, I would only ask this one if you are secure in your relationship and will not take offense at the answers you might receive. If you are this type of strong-willed individual who can take a few punches, go ahead and see what you discover.

You might be pleasantly surprised. What other people see as weaknesses, you might see as strengths. Everyone has different interpretations of what constitutes a strength or a weakness.

The person you are going to marry may turn out to be much wiser, more thoughtful, or more independent than you first imagined.

What values do you think my fiancé and I have in common?

In the book of Ecclesiastes (4:9) we find these words: "Two are better than one." The wisdom of this maxim extends to every walk of life—especially marriage.

The values that two people share don't necessarily have to produce a Norman Rockwell painting, but the common

threads of courtesy, kindness, generosity, patience, helpful-
ness, and honesty can go a long way toward creating a
relationship based on these shared understandings of life.
A generous woman will rarely find happiness with a stingy
man. A fellow who is patient and long-suffering will find
life unbearable with an impatient and short-fused woman.

Most likely, as you and your fiancé have interacted with
others, your family and friends have been able to pick up
on these common values and principles the two of you
share. They will be able to give you some valuable insights.

If you are concerned about this area of your relationship, make a list of the values and morals that are most
important in your life. Talk to your friends and see if they
believe your fiancé is guided by these same values and
principles.

Another way to gain a deeper understanding of your
fiancé's values is to review the section on spiritual and
religious practices found in chapter 1. Rephrase these questions for your friends and see if they can offer any new and
helpful suggestions.

In what ways have you seen my fiancé and I grow together?

There is something magical about riding a bicycle built for
two. One person gets to steer; the other gets to come along
for the thrill.

When I was quite young, I would ride a tandem bicycle
with my older cousin, whom I believed to be the epitome
of strength and agility. He always guided the contraption

and provided most of the power, too. The feeling of riding on the same bicycle with him was one of constant elation, of being swept along on some mighty adventure, not knowing what to expect or where he would turn or what I was going to see until I arrived at my destination. I was just a child who was along for the ride, going wherever my cousin's whims and fancies might take him.

There's something of an adventure and mystery in marriage, too. At various times in the relationship one person might be steering, the other pedaling. Sometimes the going is easy. At other times, it is like going up a hill. But both are along for the ride and the adventure.

Life is full of growth opportunities. There is not only physical growth—making our bodies stronger or more fit—but also the emotional, intellectual, and spiritual kinds of growth. Couples who grow together *before* marriage are far more likely to continue these patterns *in* marriage.

And that's where the bicycle imagery comes in. When two people are working together, fully in love and swept up in the adventure of life, it truly makes no difference who is steering or who is pedaling. All that matters is the movement itself, the experience of growing and learning. Being swept along in such a marriage is a wonderful feeling.

You never know what to expect or where you will turn or what you are going to see. But you always know where you're going to end up. And with whom.

CHAPTER THREE

QUESTIONS TO ASK HIS/HER FRIENDS

A man who marries a woman to educate her
falls a victim to the same fallacy
as the woman who marries a man to reform him.
—ELBERT HUBBARD

I f you want to find out how your partner acts when he/she is not with you, just ask a few of his/her closest friends. You're certain to gain a new perspective about and, hopefully, an appreciation of your fiancé/fiancée. We all act differently in a variety of social settings, so it stands to reason that you might learn more about your loved one by talking to his/her friends—especially those who have known him/her for many years.

Those friends whom we have known since childhood understand a great deal about who we are, what makes us tick, and how we grew up. They have funny stories, anecdotes, and family history to draw upon.

I've known many couples who were introduced by mutual

friends. These old acquaintances can be valuable voices of experience and memory should you desire to question them about your fiancé. Chances are that some of these friends have known your loved one far longer than you. Their impressions and advice could be invaluable.

The questions in this chapter can help you better understand your partner's past, his/her habits and attitudes, and, in some cases, his/her hidden self. You might discover a mysterious side of your loved one you never knew about. Or you might uncover heroic tales, brave exploits, or personal triumphs that lay hidden away in the shy, humble heart of your beloved.

In some of my counseling sessions with couples, there have been instances when one person has questioned an issue pertaining to the other's past. Couples rarely set out to hide things from each other, but often there are blind spots in a relationship where one person knows little about the other. Usually couples enjoy discussing these unexplored areas and feel a sense of relief once these issues are brought into the open. The nature of love and honesty in most relationships is such that couples naturally want to talk about all aspects of their lives with each other.

But perhaps there are moments or episodes too painful to discuss. A person who has endured sexual or physical abuse as a child, for instance, may never broach this subject—even with someone he/she loves. Those who have addictions to alcohol, drugs, or gambling may deny that problems exist—even after marriage. Talking to your beloved's friends about these issues may help you now and save you much misery later.

Not long ago I conducted a funeral for an elderly woman who had been married to an alcoholic for over forty years. Before she died she had expressed a gnawing grief that had eaten away at her soul all those years. "I wish I had known about his drinking problem before I got married," she said. "I would have waited until he got help. Or would not have married him at all."

After sighing deeply she added, "It was hell being married to an alcoholic."

Her funeral was one of the saddest ones I had ever conducted. I could not shake the image of her destructive husband from my mind. All those years, I kept thinking, she had lived in misery. And why? Such was the sacrificial nature of her great love, I suppose. But how many of us could endure such a travail, or would desire to?

As you prepare to speak to your loved one's friends, take a quick look through the questions in this chapter. Mark the ones most likely to be of help to you. Think about them. Memorize a few. And then draw them out the next time you are having dinner with those old friends, or happen to meet on the street or at work.

But one word of advice: While these questions are meant to be helpful, they are not meant to be a source of conflict between you and the one you love. The questions are not meant to be aids to spying or prying into your loved one's life. There are aspects of each of our lives that we have every right to guard and protect from others—even the ones we love.

However, the more open and honest our love is, the more fully we will allow ourselves to be known. The nature of love is vulnerability. But asking good questions is one way to explore these uncharted areas in marriage.

So, while the questions are here for the taking, please don't use them like a wedge, a spying device, or a sledgehammer. Let the questions flow more naturally from your love and curiosity. Ask the questions with good-natured concern and lightness.

If there is a friend or two who refuses to answer your questions, don't assume that your fiancé/fiancée has another relationship on the side or has some deep secret he/she is hiding from you or is talking about you behind your back. Just take it in stride and chalk it up to good friendship. If, however, you see patterns that appear bleak or disconcerting, you know that something needs to be addressed. Then you can tackle these concerns head-on.

I am not suggesting that you become a private detective or an information sneak thief. You don't have to become an international spy to use these questions effectively. Be yourself above all else. Laugh a lot. And reassure your loved one, if he/she happens to get wind of your friendly questions, that you are simply learning more about who he/she is. True love runs deeper than friendship, and there is no reason to assume mistrust or concealment. Most of all, have fun.

What does my fiancé say about me when I'm not around?

This is one of the best questions to ask your fiancé's friends—male or female. What you hear will tell you a great deal about the place you hold in another's heart.

Consider how wonderful it would be to hear things like: *He's definitely in love; She thinks you're wonderful; He's miserable when you're away; She can't wait to be with you; You are all he thinks about.*

If she is telling her friends about you, you know she loves you. When he's saying nice things about you—and you're not even there—you know he cares.

If, on the other hand, you happen to find out that he rarely speaks of you, never praises you, or dismisses you altogether when he is with his friends, you might have cause for alarm. Men and women who have nothing but negative comments about the people in their lives are rarely worth the trouble it would take to reform them. Best to cut off the relationship before you are married.

My experience has taught me that, on any given Friday or Saturday night of the week, there are plenty of people across America hanging out with their buddies and lambasting their spouses. A loved one who does not praise you in public and social settings before marriage rarely learns how to do so after the wedding.

Has my fiancé ever been a heavy drinker?

If you think you need to know more about closet drinkers or the games alcoholics play, visit your local chapter of

Alcoholics Anonymous and pick up some reading material. Many men and women are experts at hiding their drinking forays from those they would like to impress. Hopefully, however, if you know your loved one deeply and intimately, there would be no way he/she could hide such a secret from you. But it does happen.

There may be no reason to assume that your fiancé has ever had a drinking problem, but it never hurts to check. And even if you find out that the one you love has, indeed, had a history of alcoholism or substance abuse, that is no reason to automatically assume that the problem still exists. Many alcoholics are able to stay on the wagon through the help of support groups and therapy sessions. People can make radical changes in their lives. You might have found someone who has.

If you do discover that your fiancé has had a history of alcoholism, make certain that you discuss this issue. Your love and concern can be of much help, and chances are there will be a sense of relief because you are aware of the problem.

Talk to someone in an AA support group if you have concerns about this disease.

Has my fiancé ever had a gambling problem?

With each passing year there are increasing numbers of people in our society who are becoming addicted to gambling. Like alcoholism, addictive gambling can ruin a relationship and destroy a marriage. Your local library would have information about various support and therapy groups for addicted gamblers.

If you suspect that your loved one has a problem with gambling, make an effort to talk about this concern in an open and honest manner.

What is the craziest thing you've ever seen my fiancé do?

Take a peek in the *Guinness Book of World Records*, and you'll discover that people do some crazy things. In fact, every person has probably participated in a zany stunt or two at some time or another. One doesn't have to be a frat house party animal to claim a moment of insanity every now and again.

I know a fellow who ate an entire cheeseburger in a single bite and another who guzzled a school of goldfish. I know mountain climbers, motorcycle daredevils, and cave explorers. And chances are, you know someone who has pushed the edges of life and endurance, or who lays claim to a stupid human trick. Your fiancé might be one of them.

Ask some old friends this question, and you're sure to hear a few funny stories. Remember these, and you'll always have something to laugh about in your marriage.

How does my fiancé/fiancée react when he/she gets angry?

Every one of us has a point at which we become notice-ably angry, upset, or withdrawn. Some of us lash out ver-bally when we become angry; others walk away from confrontation. Still others seem always on the verge of striking back with a fist or throwing an object.

Before entering into marriage, you will want to understand how your fiancé/fiancée reacts when he/she becomes angry. Hopefully you will be able to see, firsthand, how your loved one responds to a cutting comment, a harsh question, or a joke. And you will want to know how he/she controls anger in a variety of situations.

Anger is a part of life, a needed emotion. But when anger is not vented properly, problems can arise. No one enjoys being around an individual who cannot control his/her anger, explodes at the first hint of confrontation or disagreement, or cannot listen calmly to the opinions and ideas of others.

Use the time before marriage to gain a greater understanding of your loved one's emotional patterns and habits. Talk to those who have worked, associated, or gone to school with your fiancé. Their observations will grant you a deeper understanding of how your loved one uses anger— constructively or destructively.

Should you desire to ask more questions regarding anger, here are a few others that might be helpful:

- How does he/she show anger?
- How well does he/she suppress his/her feelings?
- Have you ever seen him/her hit someone?
- Have you ever seen him/her provoke someone else?
- What is the worst side you've ever seen of my fiancé?

How does my fiancé help others?

If acts of kindness and generosity are important to you, ask about your fiancé's service to others.

I know many men and women who give of themselves immeasurably to others, who find satisfaction and meaning in volunteerism and service, but are married to spouses who care little for such acts of kindness and even regret such charity. And I have observed that many couples find a mutual gratification in serving others side by side.

I see hope for the future because I increasingly see more husbands and wives (and entire families) working together in soup kitchens, in service organizations, and through organizations such as Habitat for Humanity. You and your future spouse can do many things together to make a difference for someone else.

Consider the words of Honoré de Balzac: "Marriage must constantly fight against a monster which devours everything: routine." Taking the time to focus on someone else's troubles is one way to break the routine of constantly focusing upon the self. A great many marriages grow stagnant because of this myopic closure and fixation upon one's immediate concerns.

Ask around and find out if your fiancé has a reputation for helping others. This might be a point of enormous joy and benefit to you both.

When you think of my fiancé, what positive attributes come to mind?

As you approach a marriage, try to accentuate the positive as much as possible. Go out of your way, even, to find those affirmations that will bring you some delight and uplift your spirits. I am a firm believer that you will carry these positive feelings and vibrations into your marriage relationship. This is not magic, but common sense.

The best marriages I know are those in which two people continue to seek the positive in each other. When negative thoughts and feelings enter a relationship, there is mounting tension.

Long before your wedding date, practice a bit of this positive imaging. Seek out the people who know your fiancé/fiancée well and can put in a good word for him/her. Try to focus on all that is right and honest and valued in your relationship. This will reinforce your love and cement your bond of commitment.

If you feel that you could use some positive moments before your marriage, look through the self-help section of your local bookstore or visit the library. You are sure to find some titles that can help you accentuate your joy and expectations of love.

In what ways do you think my fiancé will change me for the better?

Marriage is the union of two incomplete and imperfect people. No one is able to do all things well or know the answers to all problems.

I like to remind couples that marriage will always bring

out the faults and cracks in our individual lives. As soon as a man and woman begin living together—squeezing from the same tube of toothpaste, sharing the same bed, eating the same foods—they will begin to recognize the faults and failures of the other. This can lead to tension.

But if a couple approaches marriage as a learning partnership, a growing experience, then marriage becomes a point of wonder and affirmation rather than a fault-finding expedition.

You and your fiancé can experience this same kind of growth and wonder. You can truly complement each other. Your strengths may benefit his/her weaknesses. And his/her strengths can help you to overcome your defects. If you love . . . and if you trust.

As you approach marriage, learning more about yourself may be one of the most courageous acts of faith. Allow your partner's strengths to complement you.

Remember: receiving from another is more difficult than giving.

Should you desire to focus on the positive attributes of your fiancé, here are some additional questions pertaining to acts of generosity and caring.

- How does my fiancé/fiancée demonstrate his/her kindness?
- How have you seen my fiancé calm someone who is angry?
- What nice things has my fiancé done for you?
- What do you appreciate most about my fiancé?

How would you describe my fiancé's values and morals?

A good marriage is based on shared understandings of life.

I know one couple in my neighborhood who has been married for over fifty years. Through this time they have not only maintained a sense of humor and a spirit of generosity, but it is evident that they have also shared common values. They have worked on Habitat for Humanity house blitzes together, have volunteered in the schools, and taught classes at the library.

Your friends and family will have some feel for the values and morals displayed by your fiancé. See if these values match your own.

As you begin to understand more about your loved one, you will also grow to appreciate his/her depth of character. Such integrity is important. You will have to count on it at many points in the future of your marriage.

What is the most memorable experience you've had with my fiancé?

Hollywood has produced a plethora of television shows highlighting the unique relationships of friends. *The Mary Tyler Moore Show*, in the 1970s, was one of the first shows to feature the friendship shared by three single women: Mary, Rhoda, and Phyllis. Screenwriters quickly discovered that single characters had much greater flexibility, and could be placed in more humorous and unique situations, than married characters. *Seinfeld* and *Friends* among others have elevated the escapades of modern singles to new comedic heights.

Your fiancé's personality, hopes, and values might be revealed in whole or in part by past escapades with friends. These friends might help you to see your fiancé in a new light. You might learn that your beloved is courageous or honest or uncharacteristically fun loving in certain situations.

Knowing about your loved one's past will help you to share the future together and enjoy life all the more. Understanding the past will help you to appreciate where you are going.

What do my fiancé's/fiancée's friends say about him/her when he's/she's not around?

This is a good question if you want to find out how much your fiancé/fiancée is respected within his/her circle of friends. Men and women who do not have the admiration of friends and associates will rarely gain a spouse's respect in marriage.

I've known a few bad marriages about which the wife has commented, "I knew he was a sleazeball when I married him, but I thought I could change him." But this is illogical. That kind of change never happens in marriage. A person who has no self-respect or admirable friendships will never be changed by a warm smile or a loving kiss at the altar.

There's an old adage that rings true in this regard: *You can tell a great deal about a person by the company he keeps.*

Consider your fiancé's friends. A good question to ask yourself is: *Do you respect them?* If not, chances are you still have much to learn about your fiancé. The relationship may not be as good as it appears to be.

If, on the other hand, you do share this respect for his/her friends, and these same friends have many accolades for your partner, you can bet you've found someone special.

How does my fiancé/fiancée act toward other women/men?

Take a few moments to remember how you and your fiancé met. Recall the circumstances. Consider the place, the talk, the atmosphere. These memories may serve as clues to the way in which your fiancé relates to the opposite sex.

Is your fiancé flirtatious by nature? Shy and withdrawn? Cerebral but talkative? Contemplative and studious? If you were attracted to his/her smile and laugh, chances are other women/men are, too. If he/she came on strong during that first meeting, most likely he/she relates to other women/men in the same way.

But not always. Perhaps you were *the one* who caught his/her eye. You are the one he/she was waiting for.

Talk to his/her friends and you are certain to find out how your fiancé/fiancée relates to members of the opposite sex.

What do you know about my fiancé's past relationships?

Don't ask this question unless you have some reason or need to know the answer. This is one subject you and your fiancé/fiancée should be open about, but if he/she has trouble discussing previous relationships, you might need to ask for help from his/her friends. In the event you have a naturally curious nature or are concerned, perhaps, about some aspect of your fiancé's past behavior (sexually transmitted diseases or infidelity, for example) then this question might be worth the risk.

You are likely to find that all is well and that your fiancé has had no stranger history of relationships than your own. Also, choose your sources wisely. You might not want to pose this question to one of your fiancé's ex-girlfriends or to a friend who is somewhat cool toward your fiancé. But you don't have to go undercover or become an investigative reporter to find out what you want to know.

How would you like to be involved in our wedding?

Having conducted hundreds of weddings over the years, I can attest that friends and family have strong feelings about their involvement in the wedding ceremony. Some friends will feel slighted if they are not asked to be included. Many family members will expect to play a part in the special day.

Ultimately, of course, you and your fiancé will have to make the final decisions concerning your wedding plans. But it never hurts to check things out with your family and friends ahead of time.

Organizing a wedding—particularly a large one—involves giving attention to a plethora of details. The people involved in your wedding party will play a crucial role. Schedules must be shuffled, conflicts must be weighed and balanced, and, often, tough decisions must be made concerning the number of people who will be included in the wedding itself.

One of the most difficult weddings I ever officiated at involved a long-distance relationship of the bride and groom. Both lived in different states, family and friends were arriving from all over the country, and the mothers were attempting to organize the final wedding plans. The entire affair was a kind of magnificent juggling act, with all manner and means of details whirling about until they came together at the last minute.

Luckily for the bride and groom, they managed to keep their friends despite the stress of it all. The reason for the wedding's success: constant communication with family and friends. And a bit of good luck.

What does my fiancé worry about?

The first time I met Larry, he was shoveling cow manure out of a deep pit. He was knee-deep in the stuff, cursing under every shovelful he chucked over his shoulder. This was the day before his wedding to Sheila, and he was feeling a bit nervous.

"This is a great stress reliever," he told me. "Ever try it?"

"Not lately," I answered.

As he continued to shovel, I asked him what he was worried about.

"Oh, lots of things," he admitted. "My chickens aren't doing so well. I lost two cows last week. And I could really use some rain on that upper two hundred and fifty acres of corn."

Such was the life of a farmer, I assumed. But he went on.

"Worst thing is," he said, "I'm not sure Sheila knows what she's getting herself into. She has this romantic notion of farming life. Peace and fresh air, quiet evenings together. I just hope she understands how much work is involved. It's got me worried."

"Just as long as you don't expect her to shovel manure," I suggested.

Larry chucked a ripe load over his shoulder and grinned. "We had a long talk a few days ago. She knows where I'm coming from. We're doing the right thing . . . don't you think?"

"Only the two of you can answer that one," I said.

Larry paused and gazed introspectively at the chicken house. "At least we can talk. We've always been able to do that."

He shoveled again. "The way I figure it . . . as long as we each know what worries the other, we'll do all right."

With that word, I went down into the pit myself. I hate to see a man shovel manure alone.

What could I do that would surprise my fiancé?

Old friends know us best. And they can always name a few tried-and-true tricks and practical jokes that will bring a smile.

Likewise, they have a genuine idea of the types of presents that we would enjoy receiving. Use this knowledge to your advantage. You might be able to pick up some wonderful gift ideas. These friends might also provide you with some valuable tips that you can use on your honeymoon or on a nice trip or for a romantic evening with your fiancé.

Other valuable questions that his/her friends might enjoy answering:

- What do you think will make my fiancé happy?
- How do you think marriage will change my fiancé?
- What do you hope you can still do with my fiancé/fiancée after he/she is married?
- What can we do together?

CHAPTER FOUR

QUESTIONS TO ASK
YOUR FUTURE IN-LAWS

Marriage is the alliance of two people,
one of whom never remembers birthdays
and the other of whom never forgets them.

—OGDEN NASH

These questions for future in-laws, more than any others, may prove to be difficult. It is not always easy to have an open discussion with one's future relatives. This fact, however, should not deter you from asking your in-laws some honest questions.

Never underestimate the impact your future in-laws will have upon your marriage . . . for better or for worse. You may not think your future mother-in-law is such a bad sort now, but how might she treat you when she finds out that, after the wedding, you and your spouse are planning to move to another state? And what about that future brother-in-law who has never seemed to like you; how is he going to treat you after you join the family officially? Or what about that one relative who is always trying to sell you life insurance or get you to vote for his favorite political candidate? It seems that every family has an eccentric uncle who is always flaunting his wealth and belittling the accomplishments of others. How will you deal with him?

While these may be important questions in your mind, you should not fret about what you cannot change. Society never stays the same. People are more transient now than ever before. Unlike the extended families of the past, most married couples no longer live in the same communities as their parents and in-laws. Families tend to live farther apart, communicate by phone, letter, or email, and rarely live under the same roof.

And, while we might lament the passing of the American family of the 1950s, it seems that younger couples today have more freedom and autonomy than was true in the past. One reason is that more men and women marry later in life than their parents did. Another is that more women work to establish a career first, and then contemplate marriage. And generally, couples today have more years of college under their belts than their parents had when they were married. Unlike marriages of the past, few marriages are arranged by parents, and most grooms no longer offer a dowry to fathers in exchange for their daughters.

For all these reasons and more, the institution of marriage has changed and will continue to change. But in-laws will always have some role and sway within the extended circle of family. And every marriage will be influenced, at least in part, by this extended circle of in-laws.

How?

Consider the following: When you get married, you will no longer have the luxury of considering *only* your own family on weekends, holidays, and get-togethers. You need to factor in your spouse's family as well. When you get married, you are inheriting another set of family traditions, expectations, and relationships. Likewise, your marriage will be affected by the desires and expectations of both your family and your *spouse's* family. A new set of people will be vying for your time, energy, and resources. And once children enter the picture, there will be a multitude of grandparents, aunts, uncles, cousins, nieces, nephews, and other family members who will want to behold your little progeny.

Whew!

For this reason most newlyweds find that the issue of time management is of central importance. I have discovered that many couples, within that first year of marriage, reach a point of contention centering on the amount of time each wants to spend with the other's family. This stress is particularly acute at holidays.

Couples quickly discover that they do not know their in-laws well enough to gauge the depth of feeling and expectation that the in-laws themselves extend to the new marriage. In other words, everyone, the couple and both sets of in-laws, brings his/her own set of expectations to weigh upon the relationship.

Unless a couple has a clear understanding of this family dynamic, there will most certainly be added stresses and strains upon the relationship. Couples need to discuss the issues of extended family before marriage, since this is one facet of a healthy relationship. But individuals would also do well to discuss some of these expectations with their future in-laws before marriage.

Hence, the reason for this chapter.

These questions are meant to provoke some honest discussion with your future spouse's relatives. These questions will not only help you to know your future in-laws better but will also give you a better perspective on your marriage relationship and the one you love.

Moreover, these questions may provide you with an opportunity to share your expectations and hopes as you become "part of the family." Keep in mind that, if you desire to receive honest and frank answers to your questions, you must first be prepared to offer that same type of openness yourself.

Ask a question. Listen. Affirm points of agreement. Offer your opinion calmly and intelligently when you disagree.

In time you will appreciate what you have learned about your in-laws, your future spouse, and the new relationships that will grace your life. And no doubt your future relatives will appreciate you, too.

How and when do you see us celebrating holidays and family traditions together?

If your future in-laws are flexible on this point, chances are you will get along splendidly. A family that can work together, plan together, and understand that time must be shared as well as valued will certainly celebrate some wonderful holidays through the years.

As you ask this question, however, be prepared to share your own vision of holiday traditions that you would like to establish. Have a good idea of the times and places that are most meaningful to you, and why. If you and your in-laws cannot reach a consensus, try to reach a compromise that will benefit both you and your spouse.

For example, you might agree to spend Thanksgiving with your family and the religious holidays with his family. Or you might agree to host a family gathering every other year.

Nothing, of course, has to be written in stone, but a general understanding of these matters is always beneficial.

Also, as you discuss family holidays, explain the history of your own traditions and why they are meaningful to you. If, for example, you have a faith different from that of your spouse's family, tell them a little about your traditions and rituals and suggest ways in which you can share these times together. Or, if a certain family event has a particular tradition attached to it, suggest ways in which that tradition can be observed by your spouse's family. You might have opinions about gift giving, meals, or vacation time. Explain these as best you can.

Finally, be aware that you and your future spouse may wish to establish your own (new) holiday traditions and family times. If the two of you have already decided how you will do this, communicate these facts to your in-laws and offer alternatives should any concerns arise. If your future relatives are flexible, they will certainly try to accommodate your needs and wishes. After all, you're new to the family.

How often do you expect us to visit?

The greater the distance between you and your in-laws, the more important this question becomes. Not only will the answer affect your pocketbook, vacation days, and weekend schedule, it will also make a marked difference in the way you see your in-laws over a period of time. If your in-laws' expectations are higher than your own, you might grow to resent frequent visits. If their expectations are lower than your own, you might get the feeling that they resent having you around when you do visit.

This question gives your in-laws an opportunity to express their need for privacy and space. Some people, when they finally get the "empty nest," are quite happy to keep it that way. They feel they've earned it. And they don't want that nest disturbed by frequent visits from family.

On the other hand, many people experience the shock of loneliness when their last son or daughter marries and moves away. Some may relish, even pine for, many visits from you and your spouse. If this is the case, then understand that you are loved and appreciated by your in-laws.

One could do much worse than that.

How often do you expect to visit us?

Now here is the other side of the issue. How often do you want his family to visit in your home? Have some idea of your expectations before you ask the question.

I know that I have been favorably blessed with wonderful in-laws. Through the years I have come to appreciate family times together—my visits in their home, their visits in mine. And I think we have an understanding and heart-felt acceptance that the doors are always open. There is never a bad time. We always appreciate the time we spend together.

But I am aware that not every family gets along as well as my own. Some people seem to inherit dreadful in-laws: the mother-in-law who is constantly bickering; the son-in-law who is incessantly asking for a few bucks; the father-in-law who belches at the table and chews with his mouth open. Oh, well, some traits can be overlooked, I suppose.

If you happen to know that you will not be able to get along well with your in-laws, talk about this fact with your future spouse. Then try to communicate your desires to your in-laws. Give your future relatives some idea of how often you would like them to visit in your home.

Once you've reached an understanding, you will all be able to enjoy and appreciate these visits to their full advantage. And best of all, there will be no surprises.

As a new daughter-in-law/son-in-law, what expectations do you have of me?

During one arduous wedding rehearsal, I happened to note that the two families were not getting along well at all. The groom's parents seemed bored, even aloof, and made no efforts to reach out to the bride's family. The bride's family (consisting of some combination of one father and mother, and three stepparents) was equally conspicuous in their standoffishness. The tension was thick, and bride and groom tiptoed on eggshells the entire evening.

As we neared the end of the rehearsal, however, I happened to overhear the bride's pointed remark to the groom: "Your mother just won't accept me. What does she expect me to be?"

I felt for this couple, but it was obvious that neither bride nor groom had had much contact with the other's parents. And maybe for good reason.

But in spite of this, I had the distinct notion that neither had made much effort to bridge the noticeable and widening gap that had formed between their families. While this was no Romeo and Juliet situation, there was obviously a need for some resolution in the family relationships. Perhaps both bride and groom would have been served well by having a discussion with their new in-laws about expectations and personalities. Each could have made an effort to help their in-laws understand who they were—their unique gifts, talents, and attributes, their hopes and dreams for the marriage. And they could have listened with equal understanding to their in-laws' fears and expectations.

Beginning new family relationships can be awkward, but open communication can make the transition smoother.

As a new in-law, what do you hope I can bring to the family?

There is no such thing as the perfect family. All relationships need opportunities for growth, change, and nurturing.

I have known many families who have benefited from

the addition of a new son-in-law or daughter-in-law. Often a new in-law brings a sense of excitement and joy to the family; people are happy to share new possibilities, dream new dreams. Aging parents begin to hope for a grandchild. Old ruts and routines (which are part of all family life) are quickly dispelled, and there is a posturing toward the future.

You, too, might have that kind of effect upon your new family. Talking about these hopes is one way of moving into a new family with assurance and a sense of support.

Whenever we visit, how much help do you expect me to provide around the house?

You won't regret discussing this issue with your new in-laws. Some families prefer to entertain guests (even if it is you and your spouse), and some prefer to receive cooperation and help from their guests. These expectations may also vary according to the length of stay, number of children, or the amount of in-house work required to make your stay comfortable and enjoyable.

Consider, for example, such issues as cooking and cleanup. Will your in-laws expect the two of you to help with cooking or cleaning whenever you come for a visit? Would they like you to make the beds or clean up in the bathroom?

Perhaps these are not major issues for most families, but they can become points of conflict, especially during longer visits. Being aware of this potential stress is important.

Consider, also, that you can always volunteer to help with household chores—even if your in-laws consider you a guest. A little graciousness and goodwill goes a long way, especially in families.

What do you hope we can do together in the coming years?

Believe it or not, you can actually have fun with your in-laws. In addition to celebrating holidays and traditional gatherings with your new family, you might also find yourself going shopping, dining, or to movies together. Many families take vacations with grandparents, or organize weekend getaways with brothers or sisters.

One family I know has an interesting way of celebrating an annual family reunion. Each individual family unit, or clan, wears a predetermined color of T-shirt as an identifying trademark. After eating a large meal, they organize a traditional single-elimination softball tournament. Various clans pair up to take on other clans and play until one clan is declared the winner. Not being a part of this family, but having observed them from afar, I can attest that they have a great deal of fun together and have worked hard to stay in touch despite great distances and scheduling conflicts.

As your family expands, no doubt you will have ideas that will make the years ahead both meaningful and celebrative. You might even help your future spouse's family create some new traditions.

Are there any family concerns you think I should be aware of?

Your new in-laws will appreciate this question because it demonstrates empathy and a desire to be a part of the family. Wanting to know more about your in-laws—their joys and sorrows—is the first step toward growing a healthy relationship with them. You are likely to receive many answers. Perhaps you will find out that someone in the family has a health problem or is scheduled for surgery. You might discover financial concerns, emotional needs, or a clandestine history submerged beneath layers of face-saving facade. Sometimes a well-timed question can open the floodgates of discussion. Your in-laws might welcome your opinions on any number of matters.

Once you find that you have earned the trust and respect of your future family, you can certainly be of help wherever you can. Be kind and considerate. And remember—you may need some of that reciprocating consideration from them at some time in the future.

What advice do you have for me in marriage?

I consider this a great question to ask your future in-laws; it demonstrates openness, a desire to hear their opinions, and a willingness to receive the benefit of their experiences.

I have always believed the saddest people in the world are those who have closed their minds and hearts. Some people honestly believe they have nothing to learn from others, or that their learning, somehow, is complete. Education, however, is a lifelong process. Those who believe that they have achieved a pinnacle of knowledge are most certainly doomed to repeat mistakes.

As you enter marriage, look for knowledge anywhere and everywhere possible. Read as many books as you can about relationships and love. Talk to those who have been married for many years, and seek to benefit from their experiences and observations. Make a list of those aspects of marriage that you find particularly profound or meaningful—tidbits of knowledge that you would like to carry into your own relationship.

Your future in-laws might have some wonderful insights for you. They may give you some pointers, tell you how to avoid some of the pitfalls and struggles they endured, or relate some revealing insights about the nature of the person you are going to marry.

Whether you receive beneficial information or meaningless trivia, either way you will have established a bond of trust with your new in-laws. If you experience nothing else in the asking, at least you will have earned their respect.

What would you like to know about me?

If you think your future in-laws don't really understand who *you* are or what you are about, help them out by asking this leading question. They may feel compelled to ask all sorts of good questions in return.

You don't have to feel as though you are auditioning for a part, but you can reveal only as much about yourself as you desire.

I think that, on a basic level, information shared within families is a type of healthy gossip. We like to know what is happening, what makes somebody tick. We like to retell favorite stories about fathers and mothers, siblings and other relatives. The various parts of this history form a family's identity and help to shape the future.

Now that you are going to be part of a new family, help to establish your history and corpus of gossip early on. Share a few highlights from your life, maybe a few struggles, some funny episodes. Elaborate as much as possible so that your in-laws will get an accurate feel for who you are.

And remember that you never have to put on a front for anyone. Just be yourself.

What would you like for me to know about your family?

Give your future in-laws the opportunity to tell you who they are. You can make this question easier for your in-laws by asking to see family picture albums and videos, by sharing stories over a cup of coffee or while playing a board game. You might also ask to see photos from your in-law's wedding. If there are other family members present, try to include them as well.

Once you have listened for a while, try to recap the

family history in your own words and ask a few other questions which might demonstrate that you are deeply interested in becoming an integral part of the family and knowing as much about them as possible.

This is a great question to ask early in any relationship. It will bridge many gaps and help to establish an emotional bond of mutual respect.

What would you like to know about my family?

Your fiancé's family will no doubt be interested in your background and history. They will want information about your parents, brothers and sisters, where you grew up, what your family does for a living.

While it will be impossible for you to narrate your entire history, you can assure your future in-laws that you are attempting to be open and honest with them. Most families will spend a bulk of time asking questions about the past, trying to better understand each other in relation to the trials, sorrows, and triumphs of life.

I know that my in-laws and I are still asking questions after all these years. We delight in each other, have fun conversations, and grow closer as the years go by.

Giving your future in-laws an opportunity to ask about your family will also help them to feel more relaxed when the two families meet. This will be especially important if your family or your fiancé's lives far away. Talking about your family before the wedding rehearsal will also help this time to go more smoothly.

What are some of the best times you have had together as a family?

Growing up I recall going to a friend's house to look through his mother's massive collection of vacation snapshots. She had filled huge spiral binders, each bursting at the seams, with page after page of photos. As I flipped through these binders, I quickly realized that most of the snapshots were taken on the beach.

Having never been to the ocean, I was fascinated by the possibilities and excitement of such a place.

"It's no big deal," my friend told me. "It's boring. We go there every summer. I'm sick of the beach."

Years later, at my friend's wedding, I heard his mother remark with nostalgic sadness, "Vacations will never be the same. He loved the beach so much."

I never told my friend's mother about our boyhood conversation, but I did realize in that moment how important memories are within the life of any family. Every family has special moments, remembered times and places, that have become much more than nostalgia. These good times help to define the meaning of family and of love.

Giving your in-laws an opportunity to share their memories with you is an important step in your relationship. It's as if they open a door and allow you to step into their lives in a profound way.

Once your in-laws have expressed their history to you, this will also give you some great ideas about future possibilities together. Perhaps you could help them relive some of those lost and nearly forgotten good times by taking a family vacation together, spending a weekend in a state park, or simply flipping through a few scrapbooks filled with faded photographs.

What are some of your hopes for our marriage?

No doubt your future in-laws will have their opinions about your marriage, but offering them an opportunity to express their hopes will land you in good stead. Popping this question will also give your in-laws an opportunity to think about *their dreams*, too.

Many couples, of course, grow tired of hearing the most common question posed by in-laws: "When are you going to have children?" But this can be troublesome, especially as nearly half of all married couples have trouble conceiving a first child.

However, the first question will get you off to a great start with your in-laws and help you establish some solid communication. Your in-laws can play a far more important role in your marriage than you realize—and when you think about how much time you will spend together at family events, holidays, and family outings, you will want to establish a solid relationship at the beginning. And don't forget, your in-laws may also be important for future childcare and help in times of crisis.

If you do need more time to get to know your in-laws, or you feel that you could benefit from some longer discussion with them (or you just need to get to know each other better), try using some of these questions, too:

- What are some of your family traditions?
- What does your family do for fun?
- What hobbies to you enjoy?
- Are there any taboo subjects I should not discuss in the family (religion, politics, sex, etc.)?
- What have you learned about marriage that would help us?
- What is the best financial advice you could offer us?

How would you like for me to communicate with you?
This is a good question in this age when new forms of media are mixing with the old. As one generation moves from pen and stationery, another is moving to email, and yet another to text messaging. So be certain you understand what your in-laws expect—and also what is possible. Generally, you may not communicate using the same methods, but every family can learn new ways.

CHAPTER FIVE

QUESTIONS TO ASK
OUR RELIGIOUS LEADER

To the contract of marriage,
besides the man and wife,
there is a third party—Society;
and, if it be considered a vow—God.

—SAMUEL JOHNSON

N ot long ago, a friend of mine (who is also a pastor) officiated at his first wedding. Some days later he described his experience to me in a series of vignettes which he aptly titled "The Wedding from Hell."

His purgatory began and ended with the bride's mother—a verbose, overbearing woman who seemed to have an ironclad opinion about every facet of the wedding ceremony. The lighting in the church was at first too dim to suit her fancy and was later too bright. She did not appreciate the way the groomsmen stood at attention with their hands crossed over their crotches. The soloist was not singing with enough zest. The organ was too loud. The altar candles were not the right size, shape, or color. Nor did they give off a pleasing enough aroma.

At every step along the way this woman tried to take control of the proceedings, first by denouncing her future son-in-law's well-meaning suggestions as blasphemy and later chastising her own daughter for wanting to have some say about her own wedding. Each time the daughter offered her opinion, her mother took up the sword of opposition.

At one point late in the proceeding, however, the daughter refused to back down. "Oh, all right," the mother finally conceded. "Have it your way!"

As she plopped into her pew, the rest of the wedding party wondered if they had heard the last of the domineering mother. A few moments of peace and calm ensued.

However, after the bride and her father had walked down the aisle, the mother could no longer hold her tongue. "Walk slower," she demanded of them both. "People want to *see* you, for heaven's sake. This isn't a race! And you're not running to a fire!"

The poor groom, visibly shaken by this display of control and power, was guardedly optimistic about the rehearsal. "I just want to get this over with," he whispered to my friend. At last, after walking through the fire of this mother's wrath and ironclad will, the rehearsal was declared a hit (by the mother, of course), and everyone returned to their homes, relieved and satisfied that the wedding would become a reality without any further altercations.

The next day, however, minutes before the wedding was scheduled to begin, the frenzied mother appeared in the church office, full-blown panic from head to toe. "Someone's got to do something! Quick!" she demanded.

"What's wrong?" my friend asked, certain from the sound of her voice that someone had fallen and ruptured a spleen.

"It's the aisle runner," she cried out. "It's an inch too far to the left!"

Finally, having listened to this woman's insane logic long enough, my friend stopped her tirade with these words of wisdom: "Lady, whether the aisle runner is an inch too far to the left or to the right is of no consequence at all in this proceeding. This moment has nothing to do with decorations, aisle runners, or scented candles. Right now there are two people out there who love each other and want to get married before God. And no blasted aisle runner is going to make one bit of difference. God is here. I'm here. And there's going to be a wedding. So I suggest you get your fanny out there if you want to witness it!"

Angry but no worse for wear, the high-society mother made her way back to her pew and sat, stone-faced and flinty eyed, as bride and groom took their vows and exchanged rings. Everyone seemed to enjoy the wedding except the bride's mother, who tried her best to destroy what happiness could be found in the moment.

My friend later encountered the groom after the wedding and could only shake his head in contemplation of the young man's fate. His future seemed bound to the castrating mother-in-law. "The poor S.O.B. never had a chance at his own wedding," my friend reasoned. "He was doomed from the start. His mother-in-law was intent upon outdoing us all—even God—and she darn near succeeded."

I tell this story with fascination because I have always believed that a wedding ceremony is, in its essence, a simple yet profound event. Two people have gathered around them the family and friends they love the most and have asked these loved ones to witness and bless the vows that they will exchange before God.

Not all weddings (not even a few, thank goodness) turn out like the one I have just described. Most couples manage to put together a wedding ceremony that is meaningful for them, without interference, and they are able to find in the moment something of profound joy and hope that can serve as an inspiration throughout their marriage.

For most married couples, issues of faith have some relevance—even if one or the other is not formally associated with a particular religious tradition. It has been my experience as a religious leader, however, that couples often fail to ask probing questions about their faith traditions as they approach marriage. Sometimes this can lead to tension within a relationship. This tension can become more pronounced once children come into the picture.

Wise individuals will seek out the guidance of their religious leaders before entering into a marriage covenant. Often, many of the following questions can be asked within the context of a premarital counseling session and can lead to more open discussion between the bride and groom in regard to matters of faith. In addition, it helps to know something about the future spouse's religious traditions and expectations before entering into marriage. This will lead to greater understanding and help your wedding ceremony go more smoothly.

Religious professionals, while they are not usually trained counselors, can offer valuable insights that can help you in your marriage. They will also be able to counsel you as you work through faith questions, help you gain a deeper understanding of the role of faith and religious practice in marriage, or enable you to find some of the answers you may have about issues relating to your marriage.

The questions in this chapter can help you and your fiancé gain a deeper understanding of the place and importance of faith in each of your lives. Most religious leaders would welcome an opportunity to discuss any of these questions with you.

The questions in this chapter can also help to clarify the role each person will play in the religious upbringing of children and will enable one's pastor, rabbi, or other religious leader to offer guidance—especially if one is entering into a marriage with a person of a different faith or religious tradition.

Most of all, these questions will help you to know that your marriage can have meaning far beyond a piece of paper, a ring, or a name. Most religious wedding ceremonies emphasize the eternal nature of love, the significance of exchanging vows and making promises "before God." Those sessions that you share with your religious leader can assume an importance that can reach beyond the wedding ceremony itself. The emphasis will be on marriage and what this special relationship means to the two of you as you journey through life together in faith and love.

I have divided the questions into two parts. One set of questions will be of assistance if you are marrying someone within your own faith tradition. The other set will help if you are marrying someone from a faith tradition other than your own.

When you are meeting with your pastor or rabbi, keep in mind that you are planning much more than a wedding ceremony. Try to look beyond the stress and strain of such details as buying a dress, renting tuxedos, or finding a florist. Attempt to focus on your relationship and the more important questions that will shape your future.

A wedding is merely a beginning point for two people. But a marriage is for a lifetime.

You have the power to shape your marriage into a fulfilling relationship. And, in spite of the fact that life holds no guarantees, you will always have your spouse's promise to stand beside you through every twist and turn you will encounter in the future.

Take the time to discover your spiritual strength and the power of faith. These will sustain you in difficult times and help to make your marriage all the more wonderful.

Questions for
Your Own Faith Tradition

*Could you show me a copy of the wedding ceremony
and explain it to me?*

The words of a wedding ceremony are more than just
rote phrases. Every religious ceremony has a long history of
tradition and significance behind it. And so the words are
attempts to convey deeper truths about human nature, the
significance of life, the meaning of love and commitment.
Even small phrases have deeper nuances attached to them.

For example, I am fond of pointing out to couples that
the Christian wedding ceremony (at least the one I use!)
asks the question: "Will you have _____ to be your
wife/husband? Will you love her/him, honor her/him, comfort and keep her/him in sickness and in health, and for-
saking all others, be faithful to her/him so long as you both
shall live?"

The bride and groom are asked to answer "I will." These
words have a greater significance and a different ring to
them than the traditional "I do." To say "I will" rather than
"I do" implies that one is looking toward the future rather
than the past. The questions shared in the wedding ceremony are not about the past. One assumes that the bride
and groom already love each other, but that is not the question. Rather, the bride and groom are asked to make promises regarding the future: "*Will* you love?" "*Will* you honor?"
"*Will* you stand beside this person in good times and bad?"

At every step in the wedding ceremony you will be asked to make faith statements, to make vows of love and honor, to pledge your lifelong commitment and promise.

These vows are never easy—or, at least, they should not be. There is mystery and joy in the words of every ceremony, a posture of divine truth. As such it is important that you and your fiancé understand the wedding ceremony which you have chosen.

Also, a copy of the words of the wedding ceremony makes a wonderful keepsake. Ask your pastor or rabbi to provide a clean copy for you so that you and your fiancé might make reference to your vows and promises each year on the date of your anniversary.

What advice do you normally give to couples contemplating marriage?

Henry Mayhew penned these words in 1845: "Advice to persons about to marry—Don't."

We can laugh at such advice, of course, because we know that great marriages do happen . . . with much work. Of course we expect our own to be wonderful. But marriage is never easy, even though the benefits far outweigh the adversities.

Every pastor or rabbi will have a few tidbits of wisdom that he/she would love to pass along to you. Some of this advice may revolve around issues of communication and faithfulness. Other advice might emphasize the elements of faith and love. I often discuss these things, too, but tend to focus on the practical aspects of marriage when asked for my advice.

For example, I tell couples, as my mother told me, that in marriage they will find themselves arguing or disagreeing about three things: sex, time, and money, but not necessarily in that order. They will not always agree about sex because there will be moments when one of them will want to make love and the other one will not, or one of them will want to start a family and the other one will not. They will disagree about how to spend their time because one of them will want to go in a certain direction and the other one will want to do something else. And they will argue about money because typically one of them will be a spender and the other one a saver.

These observations may not be universally true, but my experience with married couples has taught me that they are not far from the reality experienced in most marriages.

In marriage, embrace every good bit of advice you can find. Talk to each other about your problems and concerns and you'll find that the best in life seems to come your way.

Do you know of any support groups for newly married couples?

If you find that you have fewer friends after marriage, or don't seem to relate as well to your single friends, don't despair. Work at finding new friendships with other couples who share your interests and values.

Often these support groups can be found through your church, synagogue, or mosque. You might also find new friendships through sports leagues, community projects, or special-interest gatherings.

While a support group might not seem so important at the beginning of your marriage, I think you will find that good friendships can make a difference to your future. The more friends you have, the greater is your support network.

What does this faith teach about the nature of marriage?

Every faith has a theology of marriage. This theology, if you both embrace it, can help the two of you to live more fully, to find spiritual as well as physical and emotional closeness, and to sense the presence of God in your marriage.

Erich Fromm, in *The Art of Loving*, wrote, "To love means to commit oneself without guarantee, to give oneself completely in the hope that our love will produce love in the loved person. Love is an act of faith."

Marital closeness does not happen by accident but is achieved only if two people create time and space for each other. As you speak with your spiritual leader, you will find that much of what you seek in marriage does have a spiritual dimension. Your religious leader can also recommend books or videos that might be helpful to you in your spiritual journey of love.

What guidelines can help us to have a successful, life-long marriage?

I remember going to see my pastor before I was married. And, although I don't remember much of what he said, I do happen to recall a few important guidelines he passed along that have resonated in my mind all these years.

First, he talked about individuality and the need for each person, even in marriage, to be an individual first. What he meant is that marriage should never consume one person or the other but should be a means of continued growth and enhancement for both. Too often in marriage, one person always gets his/her way, while the other must sacrifice or suffer. This can lead to bitter feelings. Marriage should be a sharing between two individuals.

My pastor also talked about forgiveness being the cornerstone of the relationship. How true this has turned out to be in my own marriage! I have often made mistakes, and so has my wife, but we have always forgiven each other. This ability to forfeit our pride, to not insist upon being right all the time, has brought us closer together over the years.

When you speak to your pastor or rabbi, I know that you will receive some wonderful guidelines for your marriage. Write them down. Keep them close to your heart. And try, to the best of your ability, to live them each day.

If we experience trouble in our marriage, where and when should we seek help?
Another observation about marriage: Many couples wait too long to seek help when they begin to experience tension in the relationship. I have known many couples who had already decided to divorce before they would agree to

go to a marriage counselor. But by this time, it is usually too late.

Help must be sought when the problem begins to creep into the relationship, when both you and your spouse are still speaking and trying to work with each other. Do not wait until you both have agreed to separate to discuss the need for counseling. If you begin to sense a problem in your marriage, quickly bring the concern into the open and discuss it.

In my experience there are several reasons why couples typically wait too long before seeking professional help. Often someone in the relationship refuses to admit there *is* a problem. This inability to reach a consensus makes it difficult to begin any discussion and can produce the seeds of estrangement and loneliness inherent in a bad marriage.

Sometimes a couple will not consider counseling because they do not wish to talk to a "stranger" about their problems. But it is precisely at this point that a "stranger" can help a couple the most. Family and friends are often too close to the source of the problem to be of any value to the marriage. Sides are taken, lines are drawn, and there is no possibility of finding a middle ground. A professional counselor can often cut through the layers of animosity and petty bickering, and help a couple to find the true source of their problem.

Other couples will not consider counseling as an option because they feel it is too expensive. They are unwilling to spend money on counseling. But this is shortsighted reasoning. Most couples will spend money on hobbies or other pursuits that do not add to the marriage, or they will allocate funds to stay in top physical condition. But a marital problem is like a tumor. It eats away at the marriage until the relationship is dead. But if a couple can spot the disease early, and agree that it needs to be eradicated, then the tumor that is festering in the relationship can be extracted from the marriage. Fixing a marital problem requires the same attention and expense as eradicating a physical tumor.

If you have a problem in your relationship, don't wait until after you are married to address it. Speak to your pastor or rabbi about counseling options. He/she will likely have a file of recommended therapists for referral.

Questions If You Are Entering Another Faith

Are there gender-related standards (e.g., no contraceptives, no job outside the home, religious obligations) that I will be expected to follow in this faith?
Never assume that you know about another faith until you have asked many questions, read official material, and talked with a cross section of adherents. You will want to explore a new faith deeply and comprehensively.

If you think you might embrace the faith of your spouse,

take the first step and talk to a leader who can articulate the various tenets of the religion in a clear and concise fashion. Ask the questions that concern *you* and will affect *you*. Try to observe how other men and women live within the faith and, if possible, ask these people about the practical implications of the religion.

I know that, as a pastor, I always feel better about the person who comes into the church asking a lot of questions. Those who accept any religion blindly will be sorely disappointed and unhappy later. I think I speak for all religious leaders when I say it is better to embrace a faith because you truly believe and can live with your questions and doubts than to have no questions at all.

How does your faith tradition differ from my own?

One of my seminary professors used to say, "If you know one religion, you don't know any." Indeed, it is true that we will never know our own faith tradition fully until we know how it differs and compares to other faiths.

If you find yourself talking to a religious leader about this issue, state your own beliefs as clearly as possible, and then ask the leader to tell you how his/her faith is similar or different. Even if you don't agree (and religious folks rarely do—even in the same faith tradition!), you are certain to learn a few things about yourself and others.

I know that, over the years, I have grown to appreciate the beliefs in other religions and faith traditions. Even though I am a Christian (and more specifically, a United Methodist), I know that my faith and tradition does not encompass *all* truth. Moreover, I have grown in my own understanding as I have engaged in dialogue with people of other religions and beliefs, and have grown to appreciate the spiritual truths they have to offer me.

Even when people of faith disagree, there is still no reason why we cannot work together for the good of humanity. That is a truth, I believe, that all people of faith can share.

How/when do children become part of this religious community?

Once you have children, the answer to this question may dictate the level of your involvement in your church, synagogue, or mosque. Generally I have found that couples want to participate in religious activities that involve the entire family.

In most religious communities children have a special place and are cherished as gifts of God. However, the ways in which children are recognized and embraced by the community varies from faith to faith. Some Christian communities, for example, dedicate children. Other Christians baptize infants. Jewish boys are circumcised (not primarily as a medical procedure but as a religious ritual) on the eighth day after birth. This circumcision is a sign of the divine covenant that was given to Abraham and Sarah centuries ago. There are also Bar Mitzvahs for adolescent boys and, in Reformed and Conservative Jewish traditions, Bat Mitzvahs for girls. Likewise, Islam, Hinduism, and Buddhism also have special rites of passage for infants, children, and adolescents.

Ask other families in the religious community to tell you about the activities and rituals that are meaningful to them.

What advice would you give us for rearing children in an interfaith marriage?

I have known many interfaith marriages that have worked well. And a key ingredient in the marriage has been an understanding of how children will be taught and reared in faith.

For example, one couple I know (he is Jewish, she is Christian) came to a resolution at the beginning of their marriage that they would rear their children in the Jewish faith. Another couple decided that they would try to combine aspects of the two faiths, exposing their children to each tradition, and then allow them to decide for themselves once they reached the early teen years.

This second approach, obviously, is more difficult to pull off well, but perhaps it can be done if both parents are open and honest about their own feelings and expectations. Either way, a religious leader can offer advice (which you might take to heart or refuse) concerning the faith issues that might have an impact on your children as they grow older.

Additionally, at some point in most faiths, there are expectations that are placed upon the children by the faith community. Children might be required to attend Hebrew classes, Confirmation classes, or other learning sessions before they can become full members of the church or synagogue. It is always a good idea to talk about these issues with your pastor or rabbi long before children arrive. In this way you can be assured of having the most pertinent information as you plan your family and future together.

Are there classes I can take, or books I can read, to learn more about this faith?

As previously mentioned, information is vitally important for understanding any faith. Your religious leader will be able to guide you to classes and reading material that can provide the information you are looking for.

Taking a college course in a particular religion is also an excellent way of learning about the history and theology of a given faith. Plus you will gain a greater breadth of knowledge by having dialogues with other students.

Most churches and synagogues also offer information sessions for those who are exploring the faith.

Will I be expected to "convert" to this faith?

If you and your fiancé are adherents of different faiths, you may want to discuss this aspect of your relationship before marriage. I know several couples who have successful marriages even though husband and wife practice a different faith. They have made their marriages work because they accept these differences, celebrate them, and agree on how they will rear their children.

Ask your religious leader, however, about the expectations of the particular faith. Some faiths will expect you to "convert"—that is, make a confession and adhere to the tenets of that particular faith. Other faiths are more accepting of differences and will be open to your participation, even if you are not a "convert."

If I do decide to convert to this faith, what will I need to do?

A nervous young man once dropped by my office to ask about the Christian faith. "Is it true," he wanted to know, "that Christians baptize in the nude?"

"Are you talking about me or the baptizee?" I shot back, hoping that he would appreciate the levity.

But he didn't seem amused. "I'm taking a class on Christian history," he said. "And I read that to be a Christian you have to be baptized in the nude."

Realizing that he was serious, I explained that early Christians did, perhaps, baptize new converts in the nude but assured him that this practice had gone out of style when people started wearing bell-bottom pants.

"So, if I want to convert," he wondered, "I won't need to strip down in public?"

Handing the young man a packet of information, I

assured him that I would try to answer all his questions and set his mind at ease about this strange faith. He seemed relieved and departed with a determined smile on his face.

Like this young man, you may have questions about a new religion. In the event that you do decide to convert to your spouse's faith, you will certainly want to discuss this decision with your religious leader.

Additional Questions

- Are there counseling resources that you could recommend to us?
- Where can we find help if we have difficulties in our marriage?
- Are there courses you could recommend?
- What advice would you offer us at this time?

CHAPTER SIX

Questions to Ask Your Lawyer

Marriage lies at the bottom of all government.
—CONFUCIUS

To understand the legal complexities of life, all we have to do is read our local newspaper. Every week there are listings of people, even friends and family, who have been issued traffic violations, who have filed for bankruptcy, or who have sued for divorce. Each day people are engaged in great legal battles of every ilk and persuasion. People go to court to solve every manner of disagreement and problem. Some of these problems seem trivial in comparison to the court cases involving murder, rape, drugs, or other hard crimes. We wonder why many of these cases have to go to court at all. And yet the courts are jammed with people bringing legal action against each other—even people in the same family, church, or community.

Consider these realities before you get married. Take the time to ponder the legal implications of your future.

Marriage, among other realities, is a legally binding institution. There are hundreds of laws regarding the various facets of marriage rights and entitlements. Couples who have been living together before marriage, who have been married previously, who have children from a previous marriage, or who wish to protect monetary assets in some fashion, especially, should consult with a lawyer before walking down the aisle.

Keep in mind that laws multiply like guppies. Within the limited sphere of this book there is no way to plumb the depths of the legal system or offer suggestions for every legal situation. That might make a fine volume in its own right. But the questions you will find here can provide a good beginning. They can help you to formulate your own concerns in the event that you do need to talk to an attorney.

As you ponder the legal implications of marriage, allow me to relate three examples of how marriage changes lives—often in ways the couples never anticipated.

Doug and Teresa

Doug and Teresa had been making marriage plans for nearly a year. Both were in their early thirties, had never married, were college educated, intelligent, and financially independent; they had worked hard in their careers and had each built impeccable credit histories. Six months before the wedding date, however, one of Doug's new business ventures began to show signs of financial distress. Two months later he filed for bankruptcy. This business failure was embarrassing to him, and so he never told Teresa about his decision.

After the wedding, Doug and Teresa lived in Doug's small apartment for a month, but Teresa was already making plans to purchase their dream house. When she went to the bank, however, she was shocked to learn of Doug's bankruptcy and found that the bank would not issue a loan because of her husband's failed credit. Even though she had a good credit history before the marriage, she had inherited her husband's situation. Angry that Doug had not informed her about his failed business before they were married, Teresa felt betrayed.

It took Doug and Teresa several months, and several sessions of expensive marriage counseling, to work through their feelings and resolve their issues. They are still hoping to buy that dream house someday.

Tom and Susan

Divorced for three years, Susan met Tom through a mutual friend. She was the mother of two small children and received a monthly child support payment from her ex-husband. After several months of steady dating, Tom and Susan decided to marry. Tom seemed the perfect match for Susan: he had a secure job, loved her children, and cared deeply for her.

A month after Tom and Susan married, however, Tom's company informed him that he would be transferring to another state. The only problem seemed to be the legal arrangement that Susan and her ex-husband had signed regarding the children. A stipulation in the divorce contract prohibited Susan or her ex-husband from moving out of state so that they both could share responsibility for rearing the children.

Susan and her ex-husband were forced to go to court to resolve the issue. The litigation was expensive, and the divorce contract had to be completely rewritten.

Sam and Rhonda

Sam met Rhonda, a widow of twelve years, at a country club Christmas party. She was beautiful, attentive, and quite wealthy. Several months later Sam made an offer of marriage but was surprised when Rhonda insisted on signing a prenuptial agreement. The reasons, she said, were obvious. Her grown children insisted that she protect her estate in the event that she died before Sam. And she was fearful that lawyers, without the agreement, would eat up much of her estate if she remarried, since, legally, she was still bound to several contracts signed by her late husband's business partners.

Sam did not understand why a woman of her age would be concerned about such matters but agreed to work out a legal contract that would satisfy Rhonda's children and her business interests. As Sam learned more about this arrangement, he felt a sense of relief that these legal matters were taken care of before marriage. He and Rhonda were able to enjoy many happy years together without the fear of any legal problems brought about by death or divorce.

While these are only three illustrations of the complexities of marriage law, there are many more that can, and do, surface on a regular basis. Perhaps you, too, have reason to consult with a lawyer before getting married.

While you may not have an estate worth millions or children from a previous marriage, there might be other circumstances in your life that would warrant a closer look at the law. If so, you might wish to consult an attorney by yourself or with your fiancé.

And, while the questions in this chapter are neither comprehensive nor exhaustive, they will provide some basic guidelines that engaged couples may want to consider or discuss together, or with a lawyer.

Also, please keep in mind that this book is in no way meant to be a legal document or source of legal advice. You will find general principles here but nothing that will stand up in court. If there are issues pertinent to your situation, please seek an attorney for advice.

From a legal perspective, what provisions should I include in a prenuptial agreement?

Prenuptial agreements have become increasingly popular, especially among the wealthy and famous. However, these contractual agreements can address a number of concerns.

Issues involving inheritance rights, children, and estates can be resolved before they are problems. There can also be stipulations regarding divorce and custody of minors. Mundane issues such as household chores may be assigned in a legally binding way in a prenuptial agreement. Even frozen sperm and embryos can be addressed.

A prenuptial agreement is certainly not mandatory for any marriage—in fact, the vast majority of people get married without such agreements. Having talked to many lawyers about these agreements over the years, I have concluded that most couples can get along perfectly well without them.

Naturally, however, you will want to discuss such issues with your fiancé. And, should the two of you decide to sign an agreement, you will probably need to do so in the presence of a lawyer.

On an emotional level, however, you may want to consider how a prenuptial agreement will affect your relationship—for better or for worse. Ask yourself some basic questions:

- Is the agreement a substitute for trust, or does it enhance our trust in each other?
- What provisions are most important to me, and why?
- In what ways will this agreement help our marriage?
- Do I want to set a time limitation on this agreement?

If you are considering a prenuptial agreement, ask your lawyer to show you some sample contracts and explain the various components. Talk to a few people who have prenuptial agreements and ascertain if, or how, these contracts have made a difference in their marriages.

How will marriage affect my assets and rights in the event of subsequent death or divorce?

If you are entering a second marriage, own a home, or have significant assets that you will be bringing into a marriage, asking this question will help you to determine your options with the help of a lawyer. Marital and divorce lawyers deal with the issue of special rights constantly. You will want to be aware of the law (which varies from state to state) and how it might affect you or your spouse in the event of death or divorce.

For example, suppose you have assets that you would like to pass along to your grown children or grandchildren. If you and your spouse divorce, or you should die, the law might stipulate that your spouse would inherit half, or all, of your estate. None of your assets, or few, would be passed on to your heirs.

This issue strikes at the heart of the marriage laws in each state and also demonstrates why people should always have an up-to-date will. A good lawyer will be able to help you understand what is at stake if you should die or divorce—two realities that people rarely want to deal with. In fact, most married people do not have a will, and this can lead to legal problems in the future.

What should I include in my will after I am married?

As mentioned above, an up-to-date will is important in any legally binding contract. Through a will, you and your spouse will have the opportunity to speak about and determine many aspects of your future, even if one or both of you should die, become seriously ill, or divorce. A will can also grant your children certain rights and privileges.

Not long ago I read about a legal case involving a British couple who were having trouble conceiving a child. After going through several rounds of tests, procedures, and drugs, the couple decided upon artificial insemination. The husband's sperm was frozen for later use, but no date was set for the insemination. A few weeks later, the husband died. When the widow requested her late husband's sperm, the courts refused to allow the procedure because the husband had left no will indicating that he wanted his sperm to be used.

Although this was a British case, the legal aspects of the situation would certainly wreak havoc in any court. And, though you may not anticipate having any such major crises in your marriage, you and your spouse would do well to prepare a basic will and testament that you can update and revise as your marriage and situation change.

How will children from a previous marriage be affected, legally, by our marriage?

Children deserve special consideration in any relationship. This is particularly crucial if one is entering into a second marriage.

I know many couples who have managed to blend children from two families with relative ease, while other couples seem to struggle as stepparents. If you are about to become a stepparent, information at a local bookstore or library might prove to be a valuable resource. You're certain to find a few pertinent titles on stepparenting, child rearing, and remarriage.

In the event that your previous spouse is deceased, your new spouse might be able to legally adopt your children, should you prefer this option. There may also be financial considerations that could affect your children if you remarry, such as a reduction in child-support payments. And there are numerous state laws that may affect your new spouse's relationship with your children in the event of your death.

If my fiancé has filed for bankruptcy before marriage, how will this decision affect me after marriage?

Like the story of Doug and Teresa in the introduction to this chapter, many people today are inheriting financial difficulties from the outset of marriage. Sometimes these financial burdens are the result of overspending or failed business ventures. Other couples simply have limited financial resources or fail to pay their debts in a timely manner.

Bankruptcy is a particularly painful decision and can mar a couple's ability to borrow for several years. If you or your fiancé has had to declare bankruptcy before marriage, the advice of an accountant or financial consultant might be invaluable to you in your first years of marriage.

How will I be affected by my fiancé's debt if we marry?
In addition to bankruptcy, mounting debt can add much
stress to a new marriage. I have known couples whose
marriages were severely strained by rising credit card bills,
who were so far in debt that they viewed divorce as a relief
from the bill collectors. There have been numerous occasions when I have visited newly married couples in their
homes and witnessed the evidence of such overspending:
huge houses with sparsely furnished rooms (or no furniture
at all), two new cars (with payments equal to many monthly
mortgages), and other high-cost entertainment items.

In addition, I have counseled many individuals and
couples who have found themselves in deep debt—often
with credit card lines of $20,000 and up (at high interest).
This kind of debt wreaks havoc on a marriage and frequently lands couples in marital counseling sessions to
deal with other issues that surface as a result of the financial woes.

I advise couples to set a strict budget before marriage,
keep their debt in check, and, if possible, begin a regular
pattern of saving and investing. In the long haul, this type
of approach will lead to greater peace of mind and happiness within marriage and will grant a couple financial
stability in the years ahead.

If your spouse has been married previously, you might
also discuss any alimony or support payments before marriage with a lawyer. By gaining a clear understanding of the
nature and legal implications of these payments, you will
be in a better position to help your marriage prosper.

How will my estate (or grown children) be affected if I marry?

From time to time I meet elderly couples who, for legal and financial reasons, have chosen to live together in lieu of marriage. Why? For fear of complicating their estates, or losing social security or pension benefits, or causing their grown children to lose some portion of their inheritance. Over the years lawmakers have sought to address many of these issues, but the law is still unclear.

Consider, for example, an older adult who has an estate of $300,000 and three grown children. There are many options for how this estate can be handled, how the inheritance can be distributed to the children.

Some people would opt to appoint a trustee for the estate—perhaps the oldest child (or the most financially dependable or frugal). This child would then make all decisions regarding the outlay of inheritance monies to the other siblings. Naturally, such an arrangement can cause ill feelings within a family, which is another reason for discussing these issues before a will is finalized.

Another person in this same scenario might opt to begin distributing the inheritance before death. The IRS (at the time of the writing of this book) allows an individual to give away $14,000, tax free, to any individual every year. This option has the advantage of reducing the total estate value over a period of time, while distributing the inheritance to heirs in smaller amounts. This might be the right choice for those people who fear that their heirs would spend the inheritance unwisely, or loaf in lieu of pursuing an education or job.

Also, keep in mind that the IRS can heavily tax an estate that is not legally blanketed by a well-written will. And the laws are changing all the time.

However, a well-versed attorney will be able to help couples, regardless of age, to work around many of these concerns and write a will that will protect inheritance and other rights for grown children or grandchildren.

How will my child-support payments be affected if I remarry?

This issue is a concern for many parents who rely upon the financial support of an ex. If a mother is raising the children alone, or is the primary caregiver, her remarriage may lower the support payments for children, thus putting a financial strain upon the new household.

Before remarriage, it would be a good idea to review the divorce contract and agreements signed before the previous marriage ended. A phone call to one's lawyer will help clear up any questions and crystallize the finer points of the divorce contract before they become larger problems.

As I approach marriage, what legal issues would be paramount for me to consider?

When Ted and Linda, both in their mid-thirties, decided to marry, they met with an attorney to discuss the legal implications of the union. Their attorney, a mutual friend, led them in a discussion of several issues that would affect their relationship—finances, assets, work, new health-related laws, living wills, children.

In the course of the conversation, Ted and Linda realized that they were in agreement on most issues. This made them feel good about their relationship and helped to solidify many of their decisions about the future.

When I meet with couples before marriage, I am amazed at the number who say, "My parents were divorced, and I remember the pain. I don't want our marriage to end that way." It seems that couples today, like never before, are aware of the divorce statistics and percentages. They don't want to become a number on a statistics sheet. They want not only to make their marriage last but to work. And that takes effort. Planning. Desire.

As one young man told me before his wedding, "We decided to talk to as many people before marriage as possible, including a lawyer. The way we figured it, it was better to talk to a lawyer before we got married than to talk to one later, if we started having problems." I was astounded by his wisdom.

No doubt a good attorney can give you a great deal of information, pose insightful questions, and bring up possible legal scenarios that are not included or suggested in any of the questions in this book. The help you receive through good legal advice may prove to be one of the most important elements in the making of a great marriage.

What legal advice would you give me about finances before I marry?

Increasingly, lawyers have had to become adept at giving financial advice—including advice on bankruptcy, debt, and even student loans. This may seem like an innocuous question at first, but if you have a personal lawyer, he or she may be able to give you and/or your future spouse many points of advice.

For example, depending on your age, a lawyer might have great advice for you about finding a financial planner, setting up an IRA (traditional vs. Roth), or funding a college education. Your lawyer might also have solid counsel for managing real estate, selling property, or various ways that you could save on taxes. A tax attorney could be especially helpful in this area.

Don't overlook the advice your lawyer can give you— and be sure to ask for advice on books, magazines, and websites (even retirement calculators, etc.) that you could reference to help plan this important aspect of your marriage.

CHAPTER SEVEN

QUESTIONS TO ASK
YOUR CHILDREN

*Marriage is a book of which
the first chapter is written in poetry
and the remaining chapters in prose.*
—BEVERLEY NICHOLS

This chapter is for individuals with children who are considering a second marriage. It is a fact of life today that many families are "blended" ones—with children from one or more marriages. And, even though the perfect Brady Bunch family doesn't exist, there is no reason why a stepfamily cannot experience and maintain love, support, and stability for all concerned.

If you are getting married again, special consideration should be given to your children. Discussing your wedding plans with them is only one facet of the changes that your children must anticipate and experience, however. Like you, they will have feelings about this new arrangement. They will have their opinions about their future stepparent. They will have their fears, doubts, and hopes about your new relationship and how these changes will affect them.

Your children will experience as much anxiety and uncertainty as you will. Sometimes they will want to talk about these issues. Other times they will retreat into silence.

Through my years of premarital counseling, I have found that men and women entering a second marriage typically have the same concerns for their children. They want to know: How can I talk to my children about my decision to marry? What should I tell them? When should I tell them? How can I help them to talk about their feelings? What should I do if my children do not want me to remarry, or do not like my fiancé?

These are all good questions, and each one deserves consideration and discussion. In some situations, all a parent needs is some quiet time with her/his children, a few moments to talk about these feelings honestly and openly. With other children, a parent will need to spend more time listening, explaining, and helping. And still other children will not want to talk about these issues at all.

Discussing remarriage is never an easy task because it demands a consideration of several other people who will be affected by the relationship.

A few years ago a friend of mine decided to remarry. But he and his fiancée had to work out a great many details, had to have several discussions with their children, before the wedding. For example, he and his fiancée each had two children from their previous marriages. He normally had custody of the children on the weekends. She had custody of her children during the weekdays. He worked at a regular nine-to-five job. She worked on an evening shift as a registered nurse in an intensive-care unit. Each owned a home. They had grown up in different Christian traditions. And their children went to different schools.

Naturally, they had much to work out before the wedding. But they were able to manage these numerous transitions because they took the time and made the effort to discuss these changes in detail. They also included the children in many of these sessions and listened to their concerns and ideas as well.

While their marriage has not been without its stresses and problems, they have managed to weave a tapestry of love through their home and have worked out all conflicts—from issues pertaining to the home, to school, to careers—by employing effective communication skills. From the beginning they involved everyone in family discussions, listened carefully to the different opinions, and worked out a plan that would be best for all.

As you read through the questions in this chapter, keep these tips in mind as you prepare to discuss these various issues with your children:

- If your children are going to be living with new stepbrothers or stepsisters, introduce the children as early as possible in the relationship. If this is not possible, bring pictures, show videos, or have a letter or email exchange to begin allowing for these new relationships to blossom.

- Allow your children to spend time with your fiancé.

- Explain, in detail and with all honesty, how your new marriage will affect your children. Some of your children's concerns might include: When will your children visit their father or mother? How many days a week will they be with you and your new spouse? Where will they go to school? Where will you live? How will your lives be different?

- Allow times and places for your children to express their feelings about your new marriage.

- Express your feelings about your new marriage to your children. Tell them why this new relationship is important to you.

- Assure your children that your love for your fiancé will never change your love for them.

- Attempt to make your children's transition as painless as possible.

As a final note, I realize that you may either be reading the questions in this chapter in the hope of using them with your own children or because you will be entering a marriage in which you will become a stepparent. Either way, I trust that the issues raised by these questions will be the beginning, and not the end, of many long talks with your children or with your stepchildren.

How would you like having _____ for a stepfather/ stepmother? Why?

Depending upon the ages of your children, the circumstances in your home, and your children's relationship to your ex-spouse, you will find that this question will provoke many feelings and perceptions. Some children may initially perceive a stepparent as a threat. They may have fears and misgivings. Other children may welcome a stepparent with joy and longing.

To be sure, the role of stepparent has taken a severe beating over the centuries. Our children's fairy tales and stories are filled with wicked stepmothers (Cinderella, Hansel and Gretel) and absent fathers (Snow White, Iron John). Furthermore, society has often maintained a stigma against the role of stepparent.

However, I have always believed every home should be regarded on its own merits. And there are plenty of caring stepparents out there who make a difference for children. You can have such a home as well. And you can help make it happen for your children.

If your children have strong feelings about your fiancé—positive or negative—try to explore these emotions as deeply and as thoroughly as possible. You might also give your partner an opportunity to express his/her thoughts to your children at some point. Having a family forum is one way to deal with deeper concerns and hopes.

How would you like having _____ for a stepbrother/ stepsister? Why?

One year at a summer camp I noticed that there were two teenage girls who seemed to do everything together. They were inseparable. At every turn they were playing on the same team, participating in the same discussion group, and sitting next to each other at the campfire.

I assumed that they were good friends, but when I asked them, they told me that they were stepsisters. "Our parents just got married," they said. "And they thought it would be nice for us to spend some time together at camp. You know, to get to know each other."

"How is it going?" I asked them.

"Great!" One of them beamed.

"We're already best friends," said the other.

This is the type of response that every parent hopes for. Not all stepbrothers and stepsisters get along so well, however. And if that appears to be the case with your children, try one or two of these ideas:

- Invite stepchildren to exchange gifts.
- Encourage stepchildren to make a list of common interests and hobbies.
- Check out a few library books pertaining to the subject of being a stepbrother or stepsister.
- Go on a family retreat together.
- Bring in a mediator if you need a third party to help your children work through their differences.

How are you feeling about my relationship with _____?

This is a good question to ask early in any relationship. Once your children have a feel for the one you are dating, they will be able to express some opinion about your loved one. Some adults actually come to value their children's opinions to the point where they can base a relationship on these feelings and impressions. I know several people who have felt drawn to another person because their children liked the individual so well.

But what if your children do not like your partner? How might you help?

First, you might ask your children to give specific examples of the reasons they do not like your fiancé. Assure them that their feelings are valid and that they need not hold anything back. Listen to your children and then attempt to give the reasons why you do like your fiancé/fiancée and why he/she would be good for you and, eventually, them.

Second, you could help to ensure that your fiancé has more time to bond with your children prior to the wedding. You could arrange for them to share fun outings, movies, or quiet times alone. You might also attempt to arrange your schedules in such a way that you and your fiancé can model a typical day for the children. Show them how you will be spending time together and what each day will be like.

Third, if your children are adamantly opposed to your fiancé, you might consider moving back the wedding date or, in lieu of such an adjustment, giving careful attention to the children during the first months of your marriage. Take the time to read as many books about stepparenting as you possibly can. Attend seminars. Talk to other couples who have made these adjustments.

How does _____ treat you?

Naturally you will want to know how your fiancé is perceived by your children. Any question pertaining to treatment or discipline can be a tricky one, but it is important to listen to your child.

If you find that your children have grown to love your fiancé/fiancée, you know that he/she has done much to foster the perceptions and good feelings of your children. Should your children express concerns, you might be able to help your partner be more attentive to the children or change an attitude or two. Some people, men especially, may not know how to relate well to children, or may feel intimidated by them. Your extra attention to this matter could ease his/her mind and greatly aid in the transition.

What do you expect from your stepfather/stepmother?

Although children may not always verbalize their feelings, or be able to, they certainly have expectations of a new stepparent. These expectations may be small: _I want him to play basketball with me; I want her to take me shopping; I want him to help me with homework._ Or these expectations can be much larger: _I expect her to always be there for me; I expect him to help pay my college tuition; I expect her to buy me a new car._

Of course, these expectations will also vary depending upon the ages of your children and where they are in life. But it is wise to discuss these expectations up front, and to continue to address the expectations as the years go by.

I believe that most stepparents welcome these expressions and feelings, and work toward fulfilling them. However, should you find some of these expectations to be unreal, or too demanding, then a heart-to-heart discussion might be in order.

What concerns do you have about my getting remarried?

Children are quite perceptive . . . and brutally honest. I know that my own children have embarrassed me many times in public with their uncensored talk and their straightforward facial expressions. But don't worry when the comments start to fly. Love conquers all. When you ask this question, your children are likely to give you some unvarnished responses.

Take the one little boy who introduced his new stepfather to me in this manner: "This is Jerry. He used to live in our basement. But now he sleeps with Mommy." If his stepfather had not been blessed with such a fine sense of humor, I don't think he would have survived the embarrassment.

Once you have told your children that you are getting remarried, they are likely to have many concerns or impressions. Like the little boy who introduced his stepfather, Jerry, as the man who slept with his mommy, some of these impressions may be humorous, others might reveal fears and hopes, even though they may seem trivial or odd to an adult. Either way, take the time to address each concern in a patient and thoughtful manner. Your child's perception of your relationship can make a big difference. You may find that you and your children have bonded in new and vital ways during the transition, and that you are able to communicate in ways you never anticipated.

Many of the issues raised by your children may be uncomfortable for you at first, but these concerns can also help you to grow. In time you will discover that you and your children have become better people by resolving many questions and concerns in a constructive way.

After I am remarried, what changes will be important to you?

Children are dreamers. They can envision all sorts of scenarios and possibilities in every relationship. When someone new enters the home, they will naturally want to hope for the best and will do all that they can to make their dreams come true.

Everyone wants and needs to feel loved, and to give love in return. Your remarriage plays a large part in fulfilling that need for your children.

Before you marry, spend quality time with your children. Talk to them about your dreams and all the possibilities your new marriage can bring. Think big, and try to help your children talk about all the changes that would make their lives better.

I know one woman (I'll call her Alice) who has made an enormous difference in the lives of her stepchildren. When the children were young, their mother was killed in a car accident. Because the children were so young at the time, they had few memories of their mother. However, when their father met Alice, the children were eager to embrace her as their "mom."

After she married the children's father, Alice not only became a mother, she also became, in their hearts, an instant celebrity and could do no wrong. It seemed that all their hopes and desires had somehow centered on her. The changes that she brought into the home were so exceptional and wonderful that . . . well, it was almost as if heaven itself had sent an angel to intervene.

All this was years ago. The children are adults now. And Alice and her husband are still happily married.

It does happen. And dreams really do come true.

Additional Questions

- What fears to you have about me remarrying?
- What expectations do you have for me?
- What is one thing I can do for you that will make you happy?
- What do you hope will remain the same after I marry?
- What do you hope will change after I marry?

CHAPTER EIGHT

SUGGESTIONS
FOR USING THIS BOOK

Thus hand in hand through life we'll go;
It's checkered paths of joy and woe
With cautious steps we'll tread.

—NATHANIEL COTTON

N ow that you have this book of questions, you are
probably wondering: How should I go about coerc-
ing my fiancé/fiancée into a corner so he/she will be willing
to talk about some of these issues with me?

Actually, it will not be as bad as all that. Hopefully you
have a relationship with someone who is accepting of your
need to discuss various topics of interest before entering
into marriage. The time you spend together in conversation not only enables you to learn more about each other
but also can be a source of laughter and strength.

Perhaps, as you work through this book with your future
spouse, you will find that the two of you do not always
agree on a given issue. If you do have disagreements, do

not despair. No relationship is without its pinch points. A disagreement is no cause to break off the relationship or throw up your hands in disgust.

Instead, use your differences to your best advantage. Recognize that there are areas that may prove to be points of tension in your marriage. This awareness may prove to be of great value to your relationship in the years ahead.

If your disagreements are important ones, try putting them behind you for a time, and then broach these subjects again at some point in the future. Time often changes how any of us sees or understands a particular issue.

Finally, as you think about communicating through the various questions in this book, try to recognize that every person has a particular personality. Your fiancé may have certain personality traits that will require your understanding and patience. But you can also try to utilize some of the suggestions below to articulate your needs and to provoke discussion. Use these helpful hints to create a setting, a mood, or a time for the perfect discussion.

You will also create healthy patterns of communication in marriage if you learn to communicate face-to-face—without yelling, judging, or interrupting. When you are talking to each other, turn off the TV, computer, and cell phones. Be in the moment together and give each other undivided attention. By doing so, you will learn how to listen well—and these skills will serve you well in the years ahead.

The Silent Partner

If you are engaged to, or dating, someone who is a silent type or tends to gravitate toward television or movie screens, sporting events, or other interests that don't facilitate conversation, don't assume that your partner has no interest in talking with you. Trying to draw a lengthy discussion out of a silent type might feel as though you are siphoning blood from a turnip, but don't give up. Try a few of these suggestions and see if you and your loved one can create some talkative evenings.

Once you have decided that you and your loved one need to converse, take a few minutes to make a list of questions. Make note of these questions (perhaps no more than a dozen), and mark them. Then go back and write them out, or type them up. Buy a nice card (or create your own) and slip the list of questions inside the envelope, along with your personal note. Mail the card or give it to your loved one the next time you step out for a quiet dinner. Realizing that you have taken the time to write out your questions, your partner will certainly wish to talk about these issues with you.

Another possibility for a silent type is to arrange a quiet evening together. Instead of going out to the usual movie or noisy sporting event, invite your loved one to spend a relaxing evening at home. Cook a meal together, order in a pizza, or play a card game. This quiet setting should enable you to ask a few of the important questions that you have gleaned from this book.

A third possibility is to help your partner ask a few pertinent questions of his/her own. While you are driving to dinner, walking across the parking lot, or standing in line, ask your loved one some leading questions such as: Have we ever talked about our families? Do you think it would be a good idea for us to talk about our finances? Is there anything you would like to know about me?

The Workaholic

When I talk to couples before marriage, I often find that one or the other is a bona fide workaholic. I have met women who were strapped to their fifty-hour-a-week shifts which required long periods of intense concentration followed by lengthy sessions of sleep. I have known men who have related tales of all-night sessions at the office and eighty-hour work weeks. Such workaholics rarely have time for discussion. And this can show in a relationship.

If your loved one happens to be a workaholic, or if you have to call his/her secretary to schedule a date, then you are probably yearning for some meaningful talk. Here are two nifty ideas for getting the kind of attention and time you will need to ask your questions.

Place a list of questions in his briefcase. Or have a florist or messenger deliver your questions along with a spray of flowers, a coffee mug, a book, or a box of chocolates. Request some time to discuss these questions over dinner or a long weekend. If possible, see if you can arrange a series of lunch meetings. Busy executives will often take clients out to lunch to discuss important issues. Follow that lead. Request some priority time with your busy executive type.

Another idea that will work for couples regardless of their personality types: Try to arrange some simultaneous vacation time. Use this work hiatus as a kind of retreat. Make it a priority during this time together to talk, question, and find the answers you are seeking from each other. If you happen to be dating a die-hard business type, you might try structuring each day around a theme or topic—with a few laughs thrown in.

Once you have secured that much-needed time together, make certain that you express your feelings about your busy schedules and your desire to find more time for each other.

The Couch Potato

Drawing discussion out of a couch potato might be easier than you think. Just arrange to turn off the television for an hour or two. One note of warning, however, for you women: This should never be implemented during *Monday Night Football* unless you want to witness a withdrawal seizure.

Once you have your fiancé's/fiancée's undivided attention, you can go to work on him/her. This should be a piece of cake (no pun intended). Every time he/she answers one of your questions to your satisfaction, feed him/her a bite of pie, a corn chip, or some other tasty delight. The more questions you ask, the more he/she is going to answer. He/she might even take to begging for some nachos. Just keep the questions and the treats flowing freely.

If this little game doesn't work with your couch potato, try another option. Sit down on the couch with him/her, open up this book of questions, and start asking the ones most pertinent to the future of your relationship. You will probably be able to ask questions all night . . . so long as you don't leave the cozy confines of the couch.

The only drawback to marrying a couch potato: You need to pay special attention to the section on household expectations and jobs. Couch potatoes are not known for their feats of daring and strength around the house. You might end up carrying far more of the chore load than you anticipate.

If you think this might be the case in your relationship, then begin with the question: How are you with dirty laundry?

The Smooth Talker

I am amazed at how many people can talk incessantly but still say nothing. Many dating relationships are based on this type of smooth talking. The problem with dating such a personality is that the relationship rarely deepens, since all issues linger on the surface. Smooth talkers are often afraid of becoming vulnerable, of opening their lives to another person. That's why they talk all the time.

Getting a smooth talker to discuss your concerns may involve some firm persuasion on your part. You may need to insist that your questions are helpful and needed, and that they should be answered with some depth of feeling and lack of concern for vulnerability.

Here are a few suggestions that might work well.

Write out a few of your most important questions and place them inside a love letter. Ask your loved one to address these questions by writing down his responses. The reason: Some people communicate more richly and deeply through writing than they do through verbal responses. Your smooth talker may turn out to be a literary giant, sharing all manner of thoughts, feelings, and hopes.

Another option involves using the telephone, fax machine, or email. You might find that your loved one can communicate much better when he/she is unencumbered or uninhibited by your presence. Naturally this may prove detrimental in a marriage (you will need to weigh this out), but if you are still dating and learning about each other, these forms of communication may prove helpful for the time being.

A third option is to confront your feelings head-on. Ask your loved one to help you work through a few issues. Ask the questions that are important to *you* and see if he/she can respond on a deeper level to *your* needs.

The Don Juan

Also known as the Casanova or the Lover, this particular type has one thing on his mind: sex. Oh, he might talk a little bit . . . in the hope that conversation might lead to something in the bedroom, but basically he is devoid of good communication skills and has a vocabulary consisting of verbs and phrases that he has gleaned from the pages of *Playboy*.

Now here's the rub (sorry). Unless you get his mind off of *your* body, you will never get to *his* mind.

So if you want to ask your questions, you're going to need some sly moves of your own. You might try the following approach. Tell him that: (1) If he will discuss some of the questions in the first chapter of this book to your satisfaction, (2) you will then agree to discuss some of the sexuality questions (which should be a real turn-on for him). This approach is akin to dangling a carrot in front of a hungry mule. You just lead him one step at a time . . . but he never quite catches up to the free meal.

A less obvious approach is to use some reverse psychology. Say something like "You know, I'd really like to talk about a few aspects of our relationship—maybe even sex and money—but I don't know if you'd be interested." No doubt his first glance will tell you: *Am I interested?! Baby, let's talk!*

Little Miss Muffet

You know the nursery rhyme. Little Miss Muffet was frightened by a spider and promptly left behind her curds and whey. But there's a lesson here: Some people are fearful of insignificant things. Others are fearful of honest talk. And in a marriage, this is a recipe for disaster. If you have a relationship with someone who seems to run away from her feelings or shy away from frank subject matter, you may need to make some new efforts at communication.

Some relationships are based upon fear and misgivings rather than love and trust. The Little Miss Muffets of the world run and hide at the first inkling of discomfort in a relationship. I have seen many. And they are not always women.

If you are dating someone who is afraid to face many of the questions in this book ("That's too embarrassing." "This is none of your business." "I can't talk about that."), you might need to help your loved one break the circle of silence. Fear is often little more than self-imposed isolation. When you love someone, there can be no room for fear.

Once you have your questions in order, consider the following idea: First, assure your partner that you care deeply for him/her. Then take the time to answer some of these questions about yourself. Show him/her by example that you *can* talk about these deep issues without falling apart or fleeing. Begin with easy questions. Proceed to the more difficult ones.

A second approach would be to give your partner this

book. Invite him/her to read through the various sections and pick out a few less threatening questions for discussion. Talk about these. Then proceed to the questions that address the issues you want to talk about.

If all else fails, check with a counselor or religious leader and see if you can't tear down a few of the cobwebs before your relationship goes any further.

The Reactionary

Perhaps you are dating, or have dated, someone who takes issue with every word you utter. This type of person might, for example, feel that a question—any question—is cause for concern. "Why would you want to talk about that?" "You mean I'm not perfect?" "You don't like me?"

If you have a relationship with a reactionary personality, try to ease your questions into the natural flow of a conversation. Preface your questions by suggesting that the two of you get to know each other more deeply. Act interested (and you should be!) in your beloved's questions and responses.

As another option, try making a game of this process. Pass the book back and forth, asking questions of each other, and see if either of you can startle the other. This may be less threatening and could open many doors of communication.

Conclusion

Regardless of the "type" of relationship you and your partner have, you can always improve your communication
skills. Consider this book a kind of practice for marriage.
Don't stop asking questions—and expecting answers—
after you have walked down the aisle. Make it a point each
day to effectively listen to your spouse, and be certain to
ask the important questions like "How was your day?" or
"What can I do for you?"

Be aware that marriage is never a 50–50 proposition—
as some suggest. Rather, marriage is a 100–100 proposition.
Marriage requires a full commitment (not half)
from both partners. This commitment begins with solid
communication—and learning how to ask good questions
is one of the foundational principles.

A FINAL WORD

I hope that as you use this book with your partner you will discover many new venues for love and trust. I hope this book can prove to be a practical guide to deepening a relationship—one that will last a lifetime. And I trust that the questions you have found in this book have proven to be helpful to you and your fiancé as the two of you prepare not only for a wedding but also for a lifetime of marriage.

No doubt some of the questions in this book are better than others. Some are more suited to your needs and situation. Others may ring hollow or seem insignificant when compared with weightier issues. My advice is simple: Use the questions that work for you. Don't try to cram all the questions into your relationship. You don't need to.

In its essence, this book is a practical guide for two people who are considering marriage. The questions in this book are meant to provoke discussion—sometimes joyfully, sometimes bitterly—but such discussions add to the depth of a marriage relationship.

Marriage is, after all (at least religiously speaking), a joining of two souls into one. When two people take their vows before God and their family and friends, they are making a declaration of great faith in each other. They are proclaiming an equality, a trust unmatched by any other institution.

The communication skills that this book can help implement will be greatly appreciated in the marriage relationship. Asking questions is good practice for marriage. These questions can brace you for the emotional and psychological battles that are part of all marriages.

I have always believed that the best marriages are those in which two people have mastered the art of love. The couples who learn to forgive, who continue to struggle through the crazy twists and turns of this thing we call life, will, in the end, find that they always have each other to lean on. This is the nature of a deep marriage. This is true love. And this is the type of relationship, the goal, toward which couples strive—knowingly or not.

So, don't give up the fight, but attempt to master the art of love. Keep asking those questions. If you do, you will triumph together.

Marriage has always been demanding, and each generation has its own challenges and frustrations to address. In spite of changing attitudes and mores, however, love has always remained as the centerpiece of marriage—and love is far more than an emotion. Love is a choice, an attitude, a way of living.

My hope is that the core of this book will teach you how to love well—and how to stay in love with each other. Little things do matter in marriage—and even a small expression of love can pay huge dividends. Keep this in mind as you grow together in your relationship and never give up the ideal of love or the dreams you have together.

Couples who can navigate through life's inevitable stresses (for richer and *poorer*, in *sickness* and in health), will discover that their love will indeed deepen through the years. Your shared experiences, conversations, family bonds, and even your failures and triumphs together will all deepen your love, respect, and appreciation for each other. Marriage is remarkable because it is a shared life—a life of hopes, dreams, and fulfillments.

Best of all, you and your fiancé will have fulfilled your greatest mission in life: that of learning how to love, of learning how to give yourself away for the sake of another. You will have made divine love a reality on earth. Or, to put it in the words of an ancient Jewish theologian, the apostle Paul:

Three things continue forever: faith, hope, and love.
But the greatest of these is love.

INDEX

In addition to writing about marriage, **Todd Outcalt** enjoys speaking to groups large and small about the marriage relationship, parenting, and many other topics. If you would like to arrange a speaking engagement with Todd, he can be contacted on Facebook or via his humorous blog on reading and writing, toddoutcalt.blogspot.com. He is available for keynote events and workshops.

Todd has also written widely on wedding preparation (debt-free and cost-saving tips), premarital counseling, and many other marital topics. His book *Your Beautiful Wedding on Any Budget* contains hundreds of money-saving tips.

Todd and his wife, Becky, have been married for thirty years and have two grown children. They live in Brownsburg, Indiana, on four acres populated by squirrels, deer, coyotes, muskrats, beavers, ducks, and an array of cats. Todd and his wife enjoy hiking, kayaking, travel, and, of course, having fun in marriage.